FILM *and* TELEVISION COMPOSER'S
R E S O U R C E   G U I D E

The Complete Guide to Organizing and Building Your Business

FILM *and* TELEVISION COMPOSER'S
RESOURCE GUIDE

The Complete Guide to Organizing and Building Your Business

By Mark Northam and
Lisa Anne Miller

ISBN 0-7935-9561-4

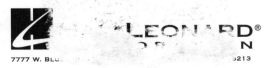

LEONARD
7777 W. BLU   3213

Visit Hal Leonard Online at
www.halleonard.com

This book is designed to provide accurate and authoritative information in regard to the subject matter covered. It is sold with the understanding that the authors are not engaged in rendering legal, accounting, or any other financial or legal services. The contracts and other legal documents contained in this book are not a substitute for consulting with an experienced attorney and obtaining advice based on the specific circumstances of a particular situation. If legal advice or other expert assistance is required, the services of a competent professional person should be sought.

The documents in this book are based on the experience of film and television composers in the United States. Circumstances, business practices, customs, and laws may make documents in this book inappropriate for use in other countries. If you are not based in the United States, you should carefully consider the business practices and laws of your country when deciding whether to use any of the documents or examples presented in this book.

Inclusion in this book does not constitute an endorsement or recommendation from the authors.

ACKNOWLEDGEMENTS

Many say that the film business is the ultimate collaboration. Without the help, coordination, and hard work of countless people, it would be impossible to create a film. Without the selfless contributions and assistance of the many people who worked with us on this project, this book would have been impossible to create. To all those who helped us, you have our deepest thanks and appreciation.

We would like to thank Steve Winogradsky for reviewing the legal documents in Section Three. Steve's extensive experience with the legal aspects of film and television music and publishing was very helpful as we prepared that section. Thanks also to Ford Thaxton for soundtrack album information, to Christine Luethje our music editor for music editing terms and information, and to Dennis Dreith of the RMA for information on AFof M union rates and policies. Thanks especially to our friend Andrew McPherson who proofread our material, and to our talented recording engineer Mick Stern for his technical contributions and wonderful attitude about music and recording.

Thanks to the "trio of Marks" for their advice and friendship — Mark Holden, Mark Lundquist, and Mark Governor.

We would like to thank all the tremendously gifted and talented musicians who have helped us in so many ways.

We would also like to thank our many friends in Los Angeles and on the Internet who have shared their thoughts and comments about what material and subjects would be important to include in this book.

Special thanks to Hal Leonard Corporation for all of their help and assistance.

Our very special thanks go to Don B. Ray, our teacher who introduced both of us to the joy of film and television scoring, and to each other. Thanks, Don!

Finally, we would like to thank our parents for their support, encouragement, and love.

This book is dedicated to those who have chosen to take the first step into a career in film and television music. We wish you the best of luck and success!

Mark Northam and Lisa Anne Miller
Glendale, California
April, 1998

TABLE OF CONTENTS

INTRODUCTION

We've designed *The Film and Television Composer's Resource Guide* to provide practical tools and information about how to organize and run your film and television music business. Most of the documents and examples in this guide have been developed over a period of years, but should not be considered final since you and your business will evolve and specialize.

It is important to note that the film and television music business is growing and expanding at an astounding rate. New broadcasting and distribution technologies are appearing constantly, and the various customs, practices, laws, and regulations that apply to the industry are constantly evolving and changing. You should consider the current state of technology, business, and legal issues whenever you choose to use any of the documents, examples, or forms presented in this guide. You should consider the appropriateness of the information presented in this guide and consider modifying it as you determine is necessary based on your own experience, geographical location, or particular situation.

In the case of contracts, agreements, and other legal documents, you should consult with an experienced entertainment attorney who can provide counsel taking into account the particular details of your situation.

The various documents, examples, and forms in this guide are intended to provide an overview of different aspects of the film and television music business, and have been organized into four different sections:

SECTION I
MARKETING MATERIALS

> This section contains marketing materials, including letters, postcards, and brochure information that can be helpful in promoting your business.

SECTION II
OPERATING YOUR BUSINESS

> The forms, documents, and examples in this section deal primarily with the production area of your business, including the management, production, recording, and delivery of music cues for film and television projects.

SECTION III
FINANCES, CONTRACTS, AND AGREEMENTS

This section shows examples of different contracts and agreements that are frequently used in film and television music projects. In this section we've concentrated on the documents that a composer may be expected to prepare.

SECTION IV
OTHER COMPOSER RESOURCES

We've included a variety of different resources in this section that may be of use to film and television music composers. Also included are internet resources that were current as of the production of this resource guide.

SECTION V
READY-TO-USE FORMS AND DOCUMENTS

Included in this section are a wide variety of blank forms and documents that are ready to be customized for your use. Information about how and when you may want to use these forms is provided in earlier sections of this book. The forms are printed without page numbers and permission is given to copy these forms for your own use.

We've included comments and notes at the beginning of each section of the guide, as well as comments on the individual forms and examples where appropriate to give as much information as possible about how the forms, documents, and examples can be used and applied to your film and television music business.

SECTION I
MARKETING MATERIALS

Marketing materials are designed to do one thing — raise your audience's awareness of you and what you're doing in the business. Marketing in this way is the heart of what some people call the *soft sell*. Let the product (in this case, your music and experience) do the selling for you. We've found this method to be very successful in breaking into the film and television music business, especially when targeting new directors and producers.

Here are the key marketing materials:

Introduction Letters — these letters can be sent to people you do not yet have a relationship with or who haven't yet met you. Done correctly, this type of mailing can raise your name awareness in the film and television business community. Although the number of projects booked directly from this type of marketing may be very small, remember the main purpose of this type of letter is for people to start hearing your name and learning about you and your music.

Demo Package Cover Letters — here's a good way to include specialized information about yourself and give your overall package a personal touch. Don't overlook the importance of this document!

Demo Tapes — your most powerful marketing tool. The way in which your tape is presented is just as important as the content. We've included information about the types of demo tapes as well as some examples of labeling.

Brochures about your Business — brochures are a great way to package all the documents you want your prospects to see or read in one impressive package. Since a brochure can contain everything from your biography to your music equipment list, it's a great way to introduce people to your entire operation.

Credits, Resumés, and Biographies — the heart and soul of your promotional materials. These are the documents that prospects will always want to look at, so we've included some ideas and samples that have worked well for us.

Postcards — a great way to keep in touch with clients, prospects, family, fans and friends. Keep them simple and to the point, and make them very easy to read. Send them when you have completed or are just about to complete a major project or when you have reached some other type of milestone or accomplishment in your career.

Newsletter — an excellent way to keep in touch with clients, prospects, fans, and others in and outside the music business. It allows you to promote yourself in a news format while keeping your readers up to date with everything you have been doing, and helps to establish yourself as an informed leader in your field.

Prospect Tracking — every composer should put together a prospect tracking system of some kind. By organizing the information you maintain on prospects into an easy-to-access format, such as a computer database, you can have the information you need at your fingertips when you need it.

Your marketing materials are your image to the business community, and in many cases first impressions about you are made on the basis of your marketing materials. By carefully constructing them to emphasize the benefits of you and your music, you can put your best foot forward each and every time you make a new contact.

INTRODUCTION LETTERS

Purpose   To break the ice and introduce yourself and your music without being too pushy or sounding like a stereotypical form letter

Recipients   Potential clients who are unfamiliar with your work or reputation

When to Use   When you are introducing yourself for the first time to people who have not specifically requested information

Description   These letters can be used to introduce yourself to people you have not met in person yet. Some composers use letters like these to do mass mailings to film-makers, music executives or anyone else in need of music. The letters should be tailored to your specific approach to the business and type(s) of music you write (score, song, etc.).

One of the most important tasks to do when marketing with letters is to follow-up with a phone call. People get dozens or hundreds of letters a day, and with the advent of e-mail and faxes they can easily suffer from information overload so will carefully choose what incoming messages and mail they spend their precious time reviewing. To make sure yours is among the *chosen*, make at least one follow-up call three days after your prospect has received the materials you sent. Continue to make further follow-up calls as necessary to make sure your materials were received and to see if your prospect has any questions or if he/she needs further information.

Believe it or not, people actually won't mind getting frequent contacts from you if you do it in a polite, constructive way. Don't get pushy — but be persistent!

Sample Introduction Letter #1

Calvin Composer
2359 Santa Monica Boulevard #911
Los Angeles, CA 90099
(310) 555-2368

Mr. Fred Filmmaker
9999 Sunset Boulevard
Suite 007
Los Angeles, CA 90099

Dear Mr. Filmmaker:

I read with interest your recent notice in [*publication, etc.*] regarding your film *Fred's Nightmare*.

If you are considering an original score for your film, I would like to speak with you. I compose music for film and television and can provide original music recorded in my own studio complete with SMPTE sync capabilities and digital audio recording.

My most recent credits include [*list a couple of your most recent credits here*].

I would be happy to send you a demo tape of music appropriate for your film or discuss any musical needs you may have. Please feel free to call with any questions or requests.

Sincerely,

Calvin Composer

Sample Introduction Letter #2

Calvin Composer
2359 Santa Monica Boulevard #911
Los Angeles, CA 90099
(310) 555-2368

Mr. Fred Filmmaker
9999 Sunset Boulevard
Suite 007
Los Angeles, CA 90099

Dear Mr. Filmmaker:

I'm sure you get lots of calls and letters from composers who all say they can write great music for you. Many of these people offer their services for little or no money, and the quality of their music often reflects this. My approach is different — I am a professional composer with national credits who specializes in providing complete music services for film and television projects, including:

- Original music composed to your specifications, including *contemporary* and *orchestral* instrumentation (using live musicians and/or electronics). I compose dramatic, romantic, action/adventure, thriller, and mystery/intrigue music, as well as comedy, contemporary and world music.

- Recording studio facilities for recording vocals and live instruments.

- Music Editing and Music Supervision services, including acquiring rights and usage licenses for all types of songs and recorded material.

- All budgets considered.

If you want a professional score for a reasonable price, I would be happy to send you a demo tape of music appropriate for your project and look forward to showing you what the *right* composer can do for you. Thanks for your time and good luck with your project!

Sincerely,

Calvin Composer

DEMO PACKAGE COVER LETTERS

Purpose To provide a quick introduction and overview of you and your services when sending a demo package

Recipients Potential clients

When to Use Whenever you send marketing materials to someone who has either:

- asked for them specifically, or
- has advertised that they are interested in receiving demo tapes or resumés from composers

Description The cover letter gives you an opportunity to add something to further reinforce your resumé, tape, and other standard marketing materials. Cover letters should always be customized to include the name and address of the person you're sending it to, along with other pertinent information such as the name of the project, if possible.

Cover letters are often read completely by the recipient, even if your tape and resumé are put in a box or stack for later review. For this reason, make sure your demo cover letter is:

- **Well written** — make sure it is easy to read and is 100% spelling and grammar checked. Just as with your resumé, credits list or bio, spelling and grammatical errors will make you look sloppy and lacking in attention to detail.

- **Concise** — be brief, to-the-point, and make it no longer than half a page (three paragraphs or fewer).

- **Informative** — mention your key selling points. This might include your latest/best credits, studio equipment, or music specialties.

- **Polite** — thank the recipient for giving you the opportunity to submit your materials, but avoid *sucking-up*. You don't want to appear too eager or anxious.

The most important thing about cover letters is that they get your message across in a direct, personal, and efficient way.

Sample Demo Package Cover Letter #1

Calvin Composer
2359 Santa Monica Boulevard #911
Los Angeles, CA 90099
(310) 555-2368

Mr. Fred Filmmaker
9999 Sunset Boulevard
Suite 007
Los Angeles, CA 90099

Dear Mr. Filmmaker:

I'm responding to your ad for a composer for *Fred's Nightmare*. It sounds like a great film and I would look forward very much to being part of your team. Please find enclosed a demo tape and information on my credits, background, and studio facilities.

I've selected the music on the enclosed demo based on what I know about your project, but would be glad to discuss any specific music needs you have for your film. I can also provide information on songs I have written if that is of interest to you.

Thanks for your time and consideration, and best of luck with *Fred's Nightmare*. I look forward to speaking with you soon.

Sincerely,

Calvin Composer

Sample Demo Package Cover Letter #2

Calvin Composer
2359 Santa Monica Boulevard #911
Los Angeles, CA 90099
(310) 555-2368

Mr. Fred Filmmaker
9999 Sunset Boulevard
Suite 007
Los Angeles, CA   90099

Dear Mr. Filmmaker:

"Oh No! Not another tape from a composer I've never heard of!! He's probably put 90 minutes of music on this tape for me to wade through! Uggh!"

I'll make it short and sweet... I'm responding to your ad for a composer because your project sounds very interesting. I'm a professional composer and enjoy doing a variety of projects from grad student films to features. I know you'll get many tapes and resumés from other composers... here's what's different about me:

1. My goal is to write music that meets all the dramatic needs of your project — whether that's a symphonic orchestral score or an all-percussion score. I work with LA's best studio musicians and many of the best up-and-coming musicians who are anxious to work on quality projects and build their resumés.

2. I can create a score to meet almost any requirement and budgetary situation. It is my desire to build relationships with filmmakers such as yourself — not extract huge sums of money on low budget projects.

I hope you'll give my tape a listen (it's about ten minutes long) and consider me for your project. I can only promise you that I will do everything I can to help you realize the full potential of your film with an original score that meets all of the dramatic needs of your film.

Thanks for your time, and good luck with your project!

Sincerely,

DEMO TAPES

Purpose   To demonstrate your ability to compose great sounding music that is appropriate for the needs of the person listening to it

Recipients   Potential clients, usually directors or television producers

When to Use   After you have established communications with a potential client and they have expressed an interest or willingness to listen to your material

Description   Your demo tape is the most important piece of promotional material you have. It demonstrates your composing, arranging, orchestration, and music production capabilities, and can be the the most important factor to a prospective client when hiring a composer. This is especially true with low budget projects and composers who do not yet have an established track record in the business.

For the purposes of this discussion, we will use the term *demo* to refer to demo cassette tapes and demo CDs. All composers at one time or another have to decide whether to use cassette tapes or CDs for demo presentations. We strongly recommend demo CDs for the following reasons:

1.   The listener can skip from one cue to the next quickly and easily. Since the listener doesn't have to go through each cue to get to the next this allows more cues to be included on the demo, and they can be longer.

2.   The sound quality is superior. There is a huge difference in sound quality between cassettes and CDs, and cassette recordings often suffer from dropouts, loss of high end, or worse yet, they might be played on a cheap boom box.

3.   CDs present a professional appearance. Like it or not, the physical appearance of your promotional materials will be considered in many cases.

There are generally four types of demos:

Soundtrack demo — this demo is an existing soundtrack album to a film or television project that you have completed. These are good for establishing yourself as an experienced composer, and the artwork and look of the album will help sell you as a professional. Use these when the film you are going after is in need of music similar to your soundtrack.

Best-of demo — this type of demo includes a sampling of different types of music. It is good for establishing your ability to write in a variety of styles, and serves to introduce the composer. Best used when you want someone to hear your music but aren't sure what type of music they may be looking for.

Style demo — this is a demo with cues in a particular style of music. Examples of typical styles are: action, animation, comedy, drama, family, horror, romance, science fiction, thriller, and western. It is always good to have this type of demo ready so that once you determine the type of music a director is looking for you can submit the appropriate music.

Custom demo — when you have specific details about what style(s) of music a director is looking for on a particular project, you may want to compile a custom demo with cues hand-picked for the project. Best used when you have lots of details about a project and you feel it is worth the extra time it takes to create a custom demo.

Your demo should look professional in all respects — don't use handwriting anywhere on the demo label or the label for the container. Make sure your phone number is clearly identifiable and don't use hard-to-read typefaces. It is also important to make sure your name is very easy to read on the side of the tape or CD. This will ensure that your demo is easy to find when placed in a stack or filed in a cassette or CD holder.

We've included some sample labels and container cards, known as *j-cards* for cassettes and *booklets* for CDs, for your reference.

Sample Cassette Label

Sample J-card

Sample CD Label

Sample CD Booklet

THE MUSIC OF
MARK NORTHAM AND LISA ANNE MILLER

FILM MUSIC SAMPLER

For information please contact CINEMATRAX at **1-888-SCORE-38**
or write to us at 6201 Sunset Boulveard #72 • Hollywood, CA 90028

For Promotional Use Only - Not For Sale

TRK	TITLE	TIME
1	Mysterious Walk	1:28
2	The Escape	:40
3	Magic Forest	3:07
4	Passport Main Title	1:19
5	Going Home	1:11
6	Simon's Chase	4:05
7	The Story	1:27
8	Space Chase	:53
9	Shooting Balloons	1:30
10	The Coffin's for You	2:43
11	Into the Sunset	1:09
12	Gotta Get Outta Here	1:44
13	Battle of the Robots	1:12
14	No Dogs Allowed Main Title	1:09
15	Jazz Balloon	2:02

(front)   *(inside)*

BROCHURES ABOUT YOUR BUSINESS

Purpose   To inform potential clients about you, your music, your credits, and your facilities in a positive, informative way. To inspire confidence in you and your music.

Recipients   Potential clients

When to Use   Since brochures contain multiple documents, they are often most effective when a potential client has requested detailed information about you and your music. They can also be effective when a filmmaker has advertised a need for a composer and has asked for a resumé or background information.

Description   You may want to give prospects some information about your studio, inventory of musical instruments, or some other details about your experience and qualifications. One way to package this information, along with your biography and credits list, is in a brochure. In addition to containing a biography and credits, your brochure can contain information and/or pictures of your studio facilities, equipment listings, and other items such as thank-you letters or success stories from satisfied clients.

Carefully choose the materials you include in your brochure, and make your brochure no more than seven pages long. Many people bind their brochures with a *Velobind* type binding (a stiff narrow strip of plastic) which works well to keep the document's shape in the mail or a *GBC* type binding (a plastic comb with many strips of plastic inserted into rectangular holes in the side of the documents). A transparent cover, along with a suitable title page and a stiff back made of card stock are nice professional touches to add to your brochure.

One important note about brochures: if your credits list is not as large or substantial as you'd like it to be, submitting it as part of a brochure (rather than on a separate sheet) can be an effective way of helping to build confidence in you and your work. The brochure allows you to highlight non-credit aspects of your business and gives you an opportunity to balance your credits with other confidence-builders such as letters from happy clients, a list of studio equipment, and other information.

Sample Brochure (cover)

THE MUSIC OF
MARK NORTHAM AND LISA ANNE MILLER
COMPOSERS FOR FILM, TELEVISION, AND MULTIMEDIA PRODUCTIONS

1146 N. Central Ave. #103 ✦ Glendale, California 91202
TEL: 1-888-SCORE-38 ✦ INTERNET: http://www.cinematrax.com

(credits list)

CINEMATRAX CREDITS

MOTION PICTURES

Cold Night Into Dawn *(starring Michael Ironside)*	Rojak Films
Guarded Secrets	Showtime
No Dogs Allowed *(starring Kate Capshaw & Rita Wilson)*	DGA/WGA Women Filmmakers
Diamonds in the Rough	Skyline Partners/Cinemax
White Balloon *(co-directed by Brian Reynolds of "NYPD Blue")*	Hank Levine FILM GmbH
Malibu Nights	Rojak Films
Running Hard	Rojak Films
Tiger *(starring Dana Plato and Timothy Bottoms)*	Artist View Entertainment
Passport	Hank Levine FILM GmbH
Skippy	Planet Earth Entertainment
Dinner	Tarquanian Productions
The Wedding Tape	Shoot The Moon Films
A Social Event	Rubba Productions
Ava's Magical Adventure *(additional music)*	Prism
The Protector *(additional music)*	Crystal Sky Productions
Beyond Desire *(additional music)*	Atlantic Releasing

TELEVISION

Beyond Belief *(weekly one-hour TV series)*	Fox Network
Wayans Brothers *(arranged and produced main title)*	Warner Brothers Network
Shopping Spree	MTM Entertainment
It Takes Two *(hosted by Dick Clark)*	MTM Entertainment
A Toucan Can *(animated film)*	Kellogg's
Crook 'n Chase	Syndicated
Hardcore TV	HBO
Wait 'Til You Have Kids	MTM Entertainment
Home and Family Show	The Family Channel
Fit TV	The Family Channel

(credits list continued)

ORCHESTRATING/ARRANGING

Orleans *(television series)*	CBS Network
Family Channel Christmas Album	MTM Entertainment
Dumb and Dumber *(animated series)*	Hanna-Barbera
Uncle Sam *(starring Isaac Hayes)*	Gable Productions
Northern Exposure	CBS Network
Meeting Phoebe	Showtime
Never Ending Story	Warner Bros. theme park (Germany)
Maverick	Warner Bros. theme park (Australia)
L'oreal	Crispen/Porter
Funny Girl	musical promo
Jekyll and Hyde	musical promo
West Side Story	musical promo

PROMOTIONAL

Married With Children promo	Guerilla TV
B.P.M.E. Open	Edifx *(formerly known as Limelite)*
WDZL News	Guerilla TV
Sound Advice	Crispin/Porter
Marinella (Mexico)	Ad Hoc Cine Y Video

THEATRE

The Scarlet Letter	Musical Director
Moscowitz is Missing	Musical Director
Interplay *comedy improv act*	Musical Director
The Seagull	Musical Director

AWARDS

BMI Film Scoring Award	
ASCAP/Fred Karlin Film Scoring Award	
Gold Addy, American Radio Advertising Federation	*"Al Bundy" (Married with Children)*
Gold Medal, The New York Festivals	*"B.P.M.E. Open" (animated film)*

OTHER

Compose and conduct for the "Writers of the Future" International Conference

(studio description)

CinemaTrax Studios

CinemaTrax Studios is a state of the art facility owned by composers Mark Northam and Lisa Anne Miller who score Film, Television, and Multimedia Productions. CinemaTrax provides both acoustic and computer based recording in a comfortable, relaxed and creative working environment.

STUDIO A

Our main studio features a full range of state of the art digital samplers and synthesizers, a Toshiba large screen monitoring system and complete SMPTE and video synchronization for digital and analog recording in a wide variety of formats. A separate studio complete with audio and video feeds is available for recording live musicians.

STUDIO B

Our second studio is designed for composing, arranging, and music editing services. Studio B is equipped with a wide variety of digital sound modules and complete SMPTE and video synchronization.

(equipment list)

Partial list of studio equipment

MIXING CONSOLE	Mackie 32 channel / 8 bus mixing console
DIGITAL TAPE RECORDERS	Tascam DA-88 including sync capabilities Panasonic SV-3700 DAT recorder Yamaha CDR-102 CD recorder Tascam DA-30 DAT recorder
DIRECT TO DISK RECORDING	Digidesign Sound Designer II Digidesign Session Masterlist CD
MONITOR REFERENCE SPEAKERS	KRK 7000B/S Yamaha NS-10M Audix A1
COMPUTER EQUIPMENT	Macintosh Quadra 650 40mb memory 6 Gigabytes of disk storage 17" color monitor Iomega Jaz 1 gigabyte data storage
SYNTHESIZERS/SAMPLERS	Kurzweil PC-88 Master Controller Roland S-760 Samplers Roland R-8M Roland JV-880 Korg 01R/W E-Mu Proteus/2 (Orchestral) ProFormance Piano module Kurzweil MicroPiano
MICROPHONES	Various, including Sennheiser, AKG
OUTBOARD GEAR/SIGNAL PROCESSING	Various, including dBx, Lexicon, Alesis, Gentner Telephone Interface with EQ
VIDEO EQUIPMENT	Mitsubishi U57 Video Recorder Sony SLV-620 HF Video Recorder Toshiba 32" Video Monitor

(thank you letters from clients)

NOTES FROM OUR CLIENTS

Thanks for doing a great job. I really enjoyed working with you.

Chris Taylor

TO; CINEMATRAX
C/O MARK AND LISA

FROM: HANK LEVINE

RE; WHITEBALLOON, CONTRACT SOUNDTRACK

DEAR MARK AND DEAR LISA,

CONGRATULATIONS FOR THE GREAT SCORE THAT YOU PRODUCED, AND THAT I LISTENED TO THE OTHER DAY. GREAT GREAT YOU ARE GREAT.

ENCLOSED FIND A SIGNED COPY OF THE REVISED AGREEMENT. PLESAE SIGN AND FAX IT BACK TO ME, AND MAIL TO MY NEW YORK ADDRESS SIGNED ORIGINAL COPYS - HANK LEVINE C/O RETO CADUFF

LOOKING FORWARD SEEING YOU AGAIN SOON AND WORKING WITH YOU IN THE FUTURE.

MY BEST GREETINGS AND WISHES FOR A GREAT AND SUCCESFUL 1997.

HANK LEVINE

(thank you letters from clients continued)

GO GIRL PRODUCTIONS, INC.

MEMO TO: LISA

FROM: PAULA & RON

Dear Lisa,

I just wanted to thank you for all of your wonderful orchestrations on our project. The tracks from the live date really sound fabulous. I know you were not feeling your best during the last couple days leading up to the studio date and I appreciate all or your effort. Please thank Mark for conducting for us and call me when you both have some time for PASTA!!!! Hope we can work together again real soon.

Peace love & blessings....

CREDITS, RESUMÉS AND BIOGRAPHIES

Purpose

To establish yourself as an experienced and accomplished composer to potential clients

Recipients

Potential clients and publicity targets (newspapers, magazines, etc.)

When to Use

When you have an opportunity to submit information about yourself based on interest in you or an overall ad to composers ("please send bio and credits to..."). Almost always sent with your demo tape.

Description

These documents are the heart and soul of your brochure or printed information package. They are usually what prospects look at first (and perhaps last!), and will often determine whether they will take the time to listen to your demo tape or not.

When you are first getting started in the business, you probably won't have a lot of credits in film and television music. A brochure or resumé format is most useful in this situation because it gives you a chance to emphasize your education, equipment or other abilities and still leave as much room as you need for credits and accomplishments.

Once you have more credits, you may want to consider a separate *credits sheet*. This spotlights your credits and allows you to focus the reader on those credits you feel best represent your work. If your educational credentials are not substantial, a *credits sheet* also solves that problem. A *credits sheet* is often sent as part of a brochure package along with photos, bios, and perhaps equipment listings, but can also be sent as an addition to a resumé.

Sample Credits List

MARK NORTHAM

MOTION PICTURES

Cold Night Into Dawn *(starring Michael Ironside)*	Rojak Films
Guarded Secrets	Showtime
Tiger *(starring Dana Plato and Timothy Bottoms)*	Artist View Entertainment
Running Hard	Rojak Films
White Balloon *(co-directed by Brian Reynolds of "NYPD Blue")*	Hank Levine FILM GmBH
Diamonds in the Rough	Skyline Partners/Cinemax
Passport	Hank Levine FILM GmBH
Malibu Nights	Rojak Films
Skippy	Planet Earth Entertainment
The Wedding Tape	Shoot The Moon Films
Dinner	Tarquanian Productions
A Social Event	Rubba Productions
Ava's Magical Adventure *(additional music)*	Prism
The Protector *(additional music)*	Crystal Sky Productions
Beyond Desire *(additional music)*	Atlantic Releasing

TELEVISION

Beyond Belief *(weekly one-hour series)*	Fox TV
Shopping Spree	MTM Entertainment
Wait 'Til You Have Kids	MTM Entertainment
Family Channel Christmas Album	MTM Entertainment
Home and Family Show	The Family Channel
Wayans Brothers *(arranged and produced main title)*	Warner Brothers
Hardcore TV	HBO

THEATRE

The Scarlet Letter	Musical Director
Moscowitz is Missing	Musical Director
Interplay *comedy improv act*	Musical Director

OTHER

ASCAP/Fred Karlin Film Scoring Award

Compose and conduct for the "Writers of the Future" International Conference

---

Mark Northam
1146 N. Central Ave. #103
Glendale, CA 91202

Telephone: 1-888-SCORE-38
E-mail: mnortham@cinematrax.com
Internet: http://www.cinematrax.com

Sample Resumé

LISA ANNE MILLER

Education

Bachelor of Music Composition, *Magna Cum Laude*
Florida State University

Certificate in Film Scoring
UCLA Film Scoring Program

Experience

CINEMATRAX, Los Angeles, CA
Partner. Started this company with my partner Mark Northam. Projects include film, television, albums, multimedia and promotional music.

LIMELITE VIDEO, Miami, Florida
Staff composer. Composed, wrote and produced post-scores for numerous television commercials, radio spots and company demos.

SESSIONE SENESE PER LA MUSICA E L'ARTE, Siena, Italy
Composer and Conductor. Composed and conducted original works for a summer music program in Siena, Italy. Numerous scores were reviewed to determine the selection of composers.

MIAMI-DADE COMMUNITY COLLEGE PIPERS, Miami, Florida
Arranger. Prepared popular music arrangements for this flute ensemble which held concerts throughout South Florida and overseas.

Awards

Gold Addy, *American Advertising Federation*
Received a local gold Addy for the production of "Al Bundy," a radio spot promoting the television series "Married With Children."

Gold Medal, *The New York Festivals*
Won a gold medal for the score of an animated short.

BMI Film Scoring Award
Awarded a Scholarship by BMI for the UCLA film scoring program.

ASCAP/Fred Karlin Film Scoring Workshop Award
This film scoring workshop is awarded once a year to young gifted composers. Participants learn about the craft of film scoring and are awarded a studio scoring session complete with some of LA's finest musicians.

Additional

Music editing using CUE music editing software
Music preparation using ENCORE and MOSAIC notation programs
Traditional and MIDI Orchestrating
Conducting and Arranging

LISA ANNE MILLER • 1146 N. Central Ave. #103 Glendale, CA 91202 • 1-888-SCORE-38

Sample Bio #1

LISA ANNE MILLER

Lisa was born in Ft. Lauderdale, Florida and studied music composition at Florida State University.   She also had the opportunity to study composition in Siena, Italy with the Sessione Senese School of Music. After college Lisa began writing music for radio and television commercials in Miami, Florida. During this time she won an Addy award for one of her commercials and a gold medal at the New York Festivals for her score to an animated short.

Wanting to write music for film and television, Lisa moved to Los Angeles to complete the UCLA Film Scoring Program. It was there she met her composing partner Mark Northam. During this time she won the BMI Film Scoring Scholarship as well as the ASCAP/Fred Karlin Film Scoring Workshop which is awarded to gifted young composers. Participants learn about the craft of film scoring and their music is recorded at a studio scoring session with a full orchestra.

For her first solo film experience, Lisa was selected to score the music for the film **No Dogs Allowed**, a Women Filmmakers Program production. The film stars Kate Capshaw and Rita Wilson and is the first in a series of films designed to promote filmmaking opportunities for women. Most recently Lisa and Mark completed the score to **Cold Night Into Dawn** starring Michael Ironside and Lisa composed the music for a new presentation of Chekhov's **The Seagull**.

In addition to composing, Lisa and Mark have organized and sponsor **The Film Music Network**, an organization dedicated to promoting communications and education among film music professionals.

Lisa Anne Miller
CinemaTrax
Glendale, CA

Telephone: 1-888-SCORE-38
E-mail: lamiller@cinematrax.com
Internet: http://www.cinematrax.com

Sample Bio #2

MARK NORTHAM

Mark was raised in Orono, Maine and began piano lessons at the age of 4 after showing an interest. Throughout his school years he studied classical and popular music and played in a variety of bands and orchestras, and elected to travel after high school and tour the country as a performing musician. During the 1980's, Mark toured the U.S. with a number of jazz/fusion music groups.

Mark first started composing music for film and television when he was asked to write for the HBO series *Hardcore TV*. In 1992 Mark moved to Los Angeles to pursue a full time career writing music for film and television projects. After the move to Los Angeles, he met his composing partner Lisa Anne Miller at the UCLA Extension Film Scoring program and was awarded a position in the ASCAP/Fred Karlin Film Scoring Workshop, a national film scoring competition.

Recently Mark worked on the nationally broadcast FOX television primetime series *Beyond Belief* hosted by Jonathan Frakes. The series, which enjoyed high ratings during its summer 1997 premier, has been renewed. Together Mark and Lisa have written music for over 15 feature films, including the feature film *Cold Night Into Dawn* starring Michael Ironside.

In addition to composing for film and television, Mark and Lisa have organized and sponsor **The Film Music Network**, an organization dedicated to promoting communications and education among film music professionals.

Mark Northam
CinemaTrax
Glendale, CA

Telephone: 1-888-SCORE-38
E-mail: mnortham@cinematrax.com
Internet: http://www.cinematrax.com

POSTCARDS

Purpose   To inform current and potential clients about your successes and remind them about you and your music

Recipients   Current and potential clients. Also, sending postcards to people unfamiliar with you or your music is effective in creating name recognition when done on a regular basis.

When to Use   When you have completed a significant project or have reached some other milestone/event in your professional life (e.g. acquisition of a new, fancy mixing console)

Description   Postcards are an effective and relatively inexpensive way to keep the public informed about what you're doing. They don't require effort to open (like a letter does), and if designed well, will convey your message quickly and efficiently to the recipient.

Some elements of successful postcards include:

- **Brief Text** — choose text to achieve a maximum impact with the fewest possible words. A brief glance should inform the reader of the key points of your postcard.

- **Use of Graphics** — people love to look at pictures, especially those which are cute or entertaining. Watch out for attempts at humor, though — this can be a very tricky area.

- **Use of Color** — even a minor detail like having a yellow spot light shine over the announcement text can make a postcard much more readable and get it noticed in a pile of mail.

Sample
Postcard #1

CINEMATRAX

is proud to have completed scores and arrangements for

Home Box Office
The WB Network
MTM
Hanna-Barbera
The Family Channel

CINEMATRAX

music for film and television
1 - 888 - SCORE - 38 ✦ http://www.cinematrax.com

Sample
Postcard #2

*the music of **CinemaTrax** can now be heard on . . .*

BEYOND BELIEF: FACT OR FICTION

Friday evenings at 8:00 on

Sample
Postcard #3

Mark Northam and Lisa Anne Miller
are proud to announce the arrival of . . .

TWO NEW SCORES FROM

CINEMATRAX

"It Takes Two"

airing weekdays at 4:30pm
on
The Family Channel

"Wait 'Til You Have Kids"

airing weekdays at 3:00pm
on
The Family Channel

Sample
Postcard #4

ATTENTION ALL SHOPPERS:

New From CinemaTrax

"SHOPPING SPREE"

Airing weekdays at 3:30 PST
on
The Family Channel

CINEMATRAX music for film and television
1-888-SCORE-38 • http://www.cinematrax.com

Sample
Postcard #5
(front)

Mr. Fred Filmmaker
9999 Sunset Boulevard
Suite 007
Los Angeles, CA 90099

(back)

TWO NEW FEATURE
FILM SCORES FROM

THE MUSIC OF MARK NORTHAM AND LISA ANNE MILLER

"**Running Hard**"
directed by Serge Rodnunsky

our latest action feature
for
Orion Films

"**Guarded Secrets**"
directed by Christopher Taylor

coming soon
to
Showtime

NEWSLETTERS

Purpose   To inform clients and potential clients about your successes, milestones, and generally what's going on with you and your business

Recipients   Clients, prospects, friends, family and fans

When to Use   Newsletters are best when done on a regular basis. The frequency can be based on your level of business activity or can be done on a calendar basis (monthly, quarterly, etc.)

Description   A newsletter is an excellent way to keep in touch with clients, prospects, fans, and others in and outside the music business. The downside of a newsletter is that it can take a great deal of time to produce, print, and distribute. The positive aspects include increased exposure to your target audience via regular mailings, and an opportunity to promote yourself in a news format as an informed leader in your field.

A recent survey found that people are much more likely to read a newsletter than a piece of direct mail advertising (flyer, letter, etc.). Newsletters also allow you to publicize the different types of products and services you offer. Clients who may know you only as a television composer may be surprised to find out the extent of film music you have written or are working on currently.

One important aspect of your newsletter should be the balance between *promotion* ("We've just completed XYZ film..."), *informative content* ("A useful new software tool we've been using is...") and items placed for *fun or entertainment* ("Our dog Lacey spent her vacation with..."). A good newsletter has all three elements in varying amounts depending on how *promotional*, *educational*, or *fun* the newsletter is intended to be. We've included a recent edition of our own client newsletter to give you some ideas. The priorities for our newsletter are promotional and fun.

Sample Newsletter

notes@cinematrax

The latest news from CinemaTrax - the music of Mark Northam and Lisa Anne Miller

KEEPING SCORE:
2 Feature Films for Mark and Lisa

We've been more than busy here at CinemaTrax, completing scores for two upcoming feature films; erotic thriller "**MALIBU NIGHTS**" (distributed by Orion Pictures) and action/comedy "**DIAMONDS IN THE ROUGH**." Although Mark and Lisa lost some sleep putting on the finishing touches, we are pleased to say they have regained their "composure." Both projects were turned in on time to rave reviews from our clients.

Mark and Lisa in the studio with the "Executive Producer"

TOGETHER FOR THE HOLIDAYS:
CinemaTrax and The Family Channel bring you Christmas cheer

As the first winter snow comes drifting down, and the smell of homemade treats fills our kitchens, we at CinemaTrax have gotten into the holiday spirit! Mark and Lisa have produced a series of Christmas on-air promos for **The Family Channel**, and have provided orchestrations and arrangements for The Family Channel's Christmas Album, featuring **Cristina Ferrare** and **Chuck Woolery**. It was such a successful "marriage" that CinemaTrax and The Family Channel are planning several special albums in the coming year. Ho! Ho! Ho!

Sample Newsletter (continued)

FILM MUSIC ON THE INTERNET!

Mark and Lisa are proud to announce the arrival of the official CinemaTrax web site now located at:

http://www.cinematrax.com

Our web site features:

- ✦ Comprehensive guide to **film music terms & people**
- ✦ **Ten questions** a filmmaker should ask a potential composer
- ✦ **ASCAP & BMI** - who are they? what do they mean to you?
- ✦ Film & Television music links
- ✦ **Directors Spotlight** - our first in a series featuring **Linda Rockstroh**, director of "No Dogs Allowed" starring Kate Capshaw and Rita Wilson
- ✦ **Downloadable music** from Mark and Lisa
- ✦ **notes@cinematrax** - our online newsletter!
- ✦ Music clearing 101 - how to clear songs for *your* film
- ✦ Surprise page with our company mascot Lacey!

SMART AND SMARTER:
CinemaTrax Does Arrangements for Hanna-Barbera

Earlier this year, Mark and Lisa arranged music for Hanna Barbera's animated TV series, "**DUMB AND DUMBER**." Even the two lead characters - though less than geniuses - were smart enough to recognize the magic in the music. Catch the fun by tuning into "Dumb and Dumber."

DIRECTOR'S SPOTLIGHT

For the first in our series of director interviews, we have **Linda Rockstroh**, director of "No Dogs Allowed" starring **Kate Capshaw** and **Rita Wilson**, which features an upbeat, light-hearted score by our own Lisa Anne Miller. Our in-depth director's interview covers Ms. Rockstroh's background as well as her personal insights into film directing and the role of music in creating dramatic impact on the screen. To tap into the warmth and wisdom of this fascinating woman, visit our CinemaTrax website (http://www.cinematrax.com.) Here you will find the complete interview along with more photos and music from "**NO DOGS ALLOWED**."

Rita Wilson, Kate Capshaw and Linda Rockstroh

<u>Sample Newsletter</u> (continued)

ATTENTION ALL SHOPPERS:
CinemaTrax Music on Every Aisle

We are pleased to announce that we have completed a score for TV game show "Shopping Spree." Produced by **Jay Wolpert**, directed by **Randy Neece**, and hosted by **Rob Pearson**, "Shopping Spree" is currently airing daily on The Family Channel at 3:30 p.m. Audience response to Mark and Lisa's exciting, uptempo score has been so enthusiastic that we have just been signed to score another Family Channel game show, "Wait 'Til You Have Kids." We'll tell you more about this in our next issue of **notes@cinematrax**. Entertainment execs and fans all agree that hiring CinemaTrax is the best deal in town!

CINEMATRAX GOES TO EUROPE

It's time for cafe au lait! The motion picture **"PASSPORT,"** featuring a dark, Western-style score by *"le monsieur and madamoiselle of film music"* - Mark and Lisa - will soon be shown throughout Europe. And shortly after the release of "PASSPORT," keep your eyes open for another European release, **"WHITE BALLOON,"** also featuring Mark and Lisa's music. "C'est Magnifique!!"

CINEMATRAX ON WB NETWORK

Hold onto your funnybone - - and tune into the WB Network. It's **"The Wayans Brothers,"** featuring those zany stars of the hit Fox TV series "In Living Color," **Damon and Shaun Wayans**. Mark and Lisa produced and arranged the theme song for this sitcom, which has been picked up for another season. Way(ans) to go!!

Sample Newsletter (continued)

LACEY'S CORNER

Woof!

"I got to go on vacation and meet a new friend (who's a lot bigger than me) named "Disaster" at the home of **Mick Stern**, our engineer. Disaster was bigger, but as you can see I still led the way!"

Lacey and Disaster

CONTEST! PRIZES! FUN!

Hey trivia buffs! Here's your chance to show your stuff! The first 5 readers who correctly answer our entertainment trivia question will become proud owners of fabulous **CinemaTrax calculators**!!   Are you ready to accept this challenge? Here goes:

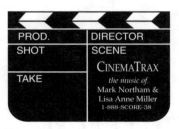

This cool looking film slate opens up to reveal a calculator inside!

NAME THE ONLY ACTOR TO HAVE PLAYED ON "PLANET OF THE APES" (TELEVISION SERIES), "STAR TREK" (THE ORIGINAL TELEVISION SERIES) AND "STAR TREK: THE NEXT GENERATION."

Feel free to invite your family and friends to play along! Send your answers to: Calculator Contest, 1146 N. Central Ave. #103 Glendale, CA 91202. If you prefer, you can e-mail us at **info@cinema-trax.com,** or simply ask Scotty to beam up your answer directly! Have fun!!

notes@cinematrax is published by CINEMATRAX
1146 N. Central Ave. #103 Glendale, CA 91202
Telephone: 1-888-SCORE-38

If you're interested in more information about CinemaTrax or music for your projects, please call us at 1-888-SCORE-38 for a demo. Be sure to ask about our free sample score offer! Happy holidays from our family to yours!

PROSPECT TRACKING

Every business needs a system of maintaining information about prospects. If you have a computer you can use database software to minimize the time required to do this and make prospect information readily available for mailings and other marketing purposes.

There are many packages available, but we consider *ACT!* published by Symantec (available on Macintosh and IBM) to be the best for our needs. It has excellent customization and letter-writing capabilities, and most importantly allows us to track every action (phone call, letter, mass mailing, etc.) we do for a prospect or client. It also has the unique capability of being able to create an unlimited number of *groups* (e.g. good prospects, great prospects, send birthday card, send latest promo, etc.) and allows for any contact to become a member of multiple groups. We've included some screen examples of our main *ACT!* database screen and the history screen.

As fast and efficient as computers are, they are still no match for a pad and pencil in some cases. We've included an example of a form you can use while *live* on the phone to jot down key prospect information. It's a good idea to keep a stack or pad of these forms handy by the phone as you make and receive calls from potential clients. It can also serve as a reminder of what information to ask for when dealing with a new prospect, and for those without a computer, this form will help get you started with prospect tracking.

Sample Prospect Tracking in ACT Database Software (Macintosh Version)

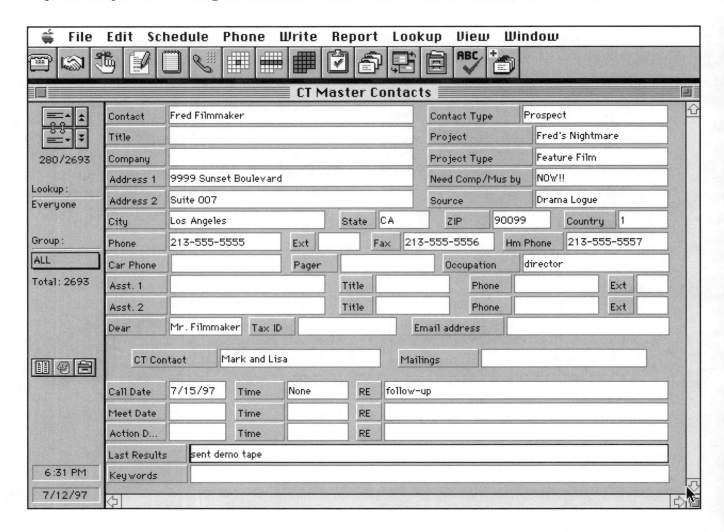

<u>Viewing the History of a Prospect</u>

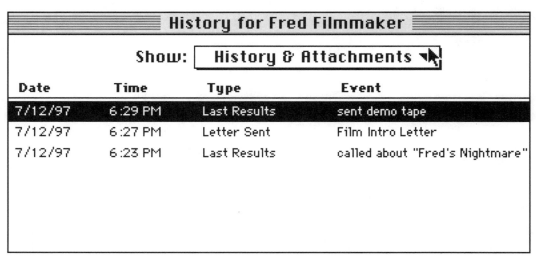

Sample Prospect Tracking Form

PROSPECT INFORMATION

Date: *Dec. 15, 1997*   Source: *Drama Logue*

Project: *Fred's Nightmare*

Contact: *Fred Filmmaker*   Phone: *213-555-5555*

Production Company: *Fred Film Works*

Address: *9999 Sunset Boulevard, Suite 007*

Los Angeles, CA 90099

Type of Project:

Independent Feature Film with video and cable release

Type of Music Needed:

Horror — electronic with some live instruments, roughly 40-50 minutes of music

Important Dates:

Rough cut ready now, final cut ready in about 2 weeks. Will have 4 weeks to score and record.

Other Notes:

Fred wants to get demos this week and meet early next week.

SECTION II
OPERATING YOUR BUSINESS

This section contains a wide variety of forms and documents you can use to manage your film and television composing business. We've presented the examples in chronological order — that is, the order you might use them during a project. Because of your individual needs, your studio or facility specifics, and the types of projects you work on, you will probably need to modify these forms. It may be best to consider them as a starting point for your own business.

Here are the forms and documents we've included in this section followed by a brief description of each. You can find more detailed explanations on the pages included with each form.

Time Code Work Tape Instructions (1/2" VHS tape) — these are a set of typical specifications for a 1/2" Hi-Fi VHS videotape with audio and visual (also known as *window burn*) SMPTE time code. With this tape you will be able to *lock* (record or play in sync) your music to picture. If you use another video format such as 3/4" U-matic, you will want to modify this document to work with your tape format.

Temp Music Work Tape Instructions (1/2" VHS tape) — this tape is used to reference any temp music added to the film, and usually contains visual SMPTE time code. The audio on the tape consists of dialogue and the temp music.

Spotting Notes — these notes are prepared during the spotting session with the composer and director. We've included examples of a handwritten spotting notes sheet that the composer or music editor might complete at the spotting session and some complete printed spotting notes documents.

Master Cue List — a list of all the cues that will be written for a film. This list is a vital reference tool throughout the composing process.

Breakdown Notes — these detailed notes are prepared by the music editor for each cue and include a variety of events that occur during the cue, such as important dialogue, camera moves,and cuts along with the time code location of each event.

Master Cue List Worksheet — we use this format of the master cue list to keep track of the progress on each cue during the composing process.

Recording Schedule — a schedule of what *live* instruments or voices need to be recorded and when.

Session Checklist — a checklist of things that should be done prior to a recording or mixing session.

Recording Session Cue Worksheet — a detailed listing of each cue to be recorded and mixed, including progress information on each. This sheet is very useful during recording and mixing as it contains reference info (time code in, out, and duration) and completion info (whether or not each cue has been recorded and mixed).

Recording Session Order — a detailed schedule for a recording session indicating what order the cues for that session will be recorded in. Working this out prior to a session aids in efficiency during the actual sessions. On the *Recording Session Order,* cues are often grouped together by instrumentation or priority.

Track Sheet — a form to indicate what has been recorded on the tracks of a multi-track tape. This document is an important reference during recording and mixing, and helps the engineer and music editor keep track of where the recorded music is located.

Performing Rights Cue Sheet — this important document is prepared after the music has been inserted into a film or television project. It documents the actual amount of music (detailed for each cue) that is used, who the composer(s) and publisher(s) are for each cue, and other important information. This document is submitted to the appropriate Performing Rights Organizations (ASCAP, BMI, SESAC, etc.) where it is used as a basis to pay Performing Rights Royalties to the composers and publishers of the music.

Final Delivery Cue List — this critical delivery document lists all of the music cues on your tape(s) and contains information about which tracks the music was recorded on and the time code location of each cue. It is used by post production facilities when working with music delivery tape(s).

Dubbing Sheet — a standard format that post production facilities use during prelay and dubbing that specifies what has been recorded on each tape track and at what time code location.

Studio Inventory — a document which lists details about each item of musical equipment, hardware, software, and any other assets of value in your studio. Maintaining an up-to-date studio inventory is important for insurance and maintenance purposes.

On an organizational note, you may want to consider creating a main work file for each project you work on. We use three-ring binders for this, and have tabs for the different sections we need, including:

- Cue list and status worksheets
- Spotting Notes
- Breakdown Notes
- Director's Notes
- Recording and Mixing Notes
- Musicians and Scheduling Information
- Synth and sampler sounds and set-ups
- Communications with clients (notes, faxes, etc.)
- Final cue sheets and delivery documents

All of the most frequently used documents are kept in this file. You may want to keep a separate confidential file for legal and financial documents. This way your project binder can be made available to anyone in the studio who needs information on the project.

TIME CODE WORK TAPE INSTRUCTIONS

Prepared By   Composer or Music Editor

Users   Composer, Music Editor, Film Production Company

Maintained   In main work file for project. Copy to music editor if requested

Description   This is a standard document we send to directors and post production personnel when we first begin a project. It specifies exactly how our 1/2 " Hi-Fi VHS work tape should be prepared with audio and visual SMPTE time code, so that we will be able to lock to picture. Since you will also need to get work tapes for your music editor, you should consult with him/her to determine their technical requirements for work tapes.

It is important to specify how you want this tape to be prepared and not to assume that the director or post production house will know what you want. Make sure to specify that any temp music should <u>not</u> be included on this tape, but that all other elements, such as dialogue and narration be included if available. Because of the varying quality of VHS video recorders, you should always request two copies of this tape - use one as your master and one as a safety copy.

If the choice and placement of source music is locked-in, you may want to ask for this to be included on the dialogue track of your work tape. If you use 1/2" VHS tape, make sure the tape is recorded at normal speed (*SP*). You also should be familiar with the two different types of audio tracks that can exist on a 1/2" VHS tape.

Hi-Fi audio tracks are the appropriate tracks to be used for your work tape audio and SMPTE time code. The tracks are indicated as *L and R* or *1 and 2*. <u>Note that audio recorded to the Hi-Fi audio tracks will not play properly on a non-Hi-Fi VHS video recorder.</u>

Linear audio tracks on VHS tape are inappropriate for SMPTE, but may be used for normal audio on the temp music tape and other non-timecode uses. The advantage of Linear audio tracks is that they can be played on Hi-Fi or non-Hi-Fi VHS recorders.

If you use another video tape format, such as a $^3/4$" U-matic, you should modify this document accordingly. $^3/4$" video tape has two audio tracks and an address track which can be used for time code. Most composers who work with $^3/4$" video tape prefer to have time code recorded on the address track.

<u>Always remember to check both copies of the work tape as soon as you get them</u>. This way you'll be able to alert the film company immediately if there is a problem and get replacement tapes delivered before your schedule becomes affected.

Sample Time Code Work Tape Instructions (¹/₂" VHS tape)

TIME CODE WORK TAPE
Preparation Instructions

Please prepare a 1/2" VHS tape as follows:

1. Record all audio except music on to the LEFT (Channel 1) Hi-Fi audio track only. Please reference signal at 0 db.

2. Record audio SMPTE signal on to the RIGHT (Channel 2) Hi-Fi audio track only. <u>Do not record SMPTE on to the analog audio tracks.</u> Please reference signal at -3db and **specify frame rate of time code. (Drop Frame, Non-Drop, etc.)**

3. Prepare window burn of time code that matches with audio SMPTE code.

Please record at least 30 seconds of time code/window burn (pre-roll) before the start of the material and 30 seconds after the end.

Please contact Mark Northam at Cinematrax at 1-888-SCORE-38 if you have any questions or if we can provide any further information.

1146 N. Central Ave. #103 ♦ GLENDALE, CALIFORNIA 91202
TELEPHONE: 1-888-SCORE-38 ♦ INTERNET: www.cinematrax.com

TEMP MUSIC WORK TAPE INSTRUCTIONS

Prepared By   Composer or Music Editor

Users   Composer, Music Editor, Film Production Company

Maintained   In main work file for project. Copy to music editor if requested

Description   This document is used to specify how the temp music work tape is to be created. This tape is used to reference the temp music (if any) that was used in the film. Having this tape will allow you to communicate with the director about the temp music and reference specific time code locations. If your spotting or breakdown notes will reference the temp music track, this tape can be used by your music editor to provide that information.

Note that there should be a *window burn* showing the time code information on the picture, but no audio time code. This tape is also referred to as a *viewing copy*.

Make sure to indicate that the video tape is to be recorded at normal speed (*SP* on 1/2" Hi-Fi VHS) for best results.

Sample Temp Music Work Tape Instructions (¹/₂" VHS tape)

TEMP MUSIC WORK TAPE
Preparation Instructions

Please prepare a 1/2" VHS tape as follows:

1. Record all audio/dialogue, including any music from the temp music track on to Hi-Fi channels 1 and 2 (L and R). Please reference signal at 0 db.

2. Prepare window burn of SMPTE concurrent with audio SMPTE code. The time code in the window burn on this tape must match precisely with the time code on any *Time Code Work Tapes* that are being provided for scoring purposes.

Please contact Mark Northam at Cinematrax at 1-888-SCORE-38 if you have any questions or if we can provide any further information.

1146 N. Central Ave. #103 ✦ GLENDALE, CALIFORNIA 91202
TELEPHONE: 1-888-SCORE-38 ✦ INTERNET: www.cinematrax.com

SPOTTING NOTES

Prepared By   Music Editor

Users   Music Editor, Composer, Director

Maintained   In main work file for project. Copies to music editor and director

Description   Spotting notes are made by the composer or music editor at the spotting session, which is a meeting where the composer and director/producer decide on music placement and the appropriate style of music for each cue.

Usually these notes are taken by the music editor or composer at the spotting session based on comments and decisions made at the session. The music editor then enters these notes into the computer and gets further information from the composer or director on any points that need clarification. Finally, the spotting notes are printed and distributed to the composer and director for reference during the project.

Different numbering systems have been developed to uniquely identify each cue in a project. Both involve using the letter *M* (indicates music) along with a number format. The two most commonly used cue numbering systems are:

1.   Three parts — first a number indicating the reel of film the cue starts in, then a letter *M*, then the order of that cue in the reel. For example, 1m1 would refer to the first cue on reel one, 2m4 would be the fourth cue in the second reel, and 3m1 would be the first cue in the third reel.

2.   The letter *M* followed by the order the cue in the entire film. For example, M1 would be the first cue of the film, and M14 would be the fourteenth. No reference is made in this system to the reel of film the cue appears on. Occasionally, a *1* will be used before the number in this system, so 1m1 would be the first cue of the film and 1m14 would be the fourteenth. This is usually done for formatting purposes to remain consistent with the numbering system described above. Some music editing programs insist on a

number before the *M*, so using a 1 in that position for all cues may be done for this reason as well.

The spotting notes serve as the basis for most of the composing efforts, and are referred to often during the project by the composer and director. The spotting notes are the official documentation of the director's wishes, and for this reason the composer and music editor should give careful attention to the details on this document.

Sample Spotting Notes #1 (form for taking initial notes)

CinemaTrax　　　　　　　　SPOTTING NOTES

Project Title **MALIBU NIGHTS**　　Composer **NORTHAM/MILLER**

Show/Prod. No.　　　　　　　　Music Editor **C. LUETHJE**

Episode Title　　　　　　　　　Length of Film/Episode

M - 1a
Start Time 1:00:00:00

"MAIN TITLE / THEME"
OVER AERIAL SHOT OF BEACH,
HOUSE - ENDS ON BEDROOM SCENE

End Time 1:01:58:24　　XFADE TO M-1B　　Total Time 1:58

Notes to Composer:

M - 1b
Start Time 1:01:58:25

"LOVE SONG"　　　(SOURCE)
OVER BEDROOM SCENE (INT.)
CONTINUES TO AERIAL BEACH SHOT

End Time 1:04:30:00　(XFADE FROM M-1A)　Total Time 2:32 (approx)

Notes to Composer: ↑ approx.

USE SONG ON TEMP?

M - 2
Start Time 1:04:32:03

"CANDLESTICK KILLING"

START ON WS OF CLIFF, BLONDE IN
BED, LISA LEAVES JAKE, BIG/FAST
OVER CANDLESTICK AND MURDER SCENE
SOME HORROR.

End Time 1:06:22:15　　　　　　Total Time 1:50

Notes to Composer:

Sample Spotting Notes #2 (notes entered into *CUE Music Editing Software*)

Production: <u>MALIBU NIGHTS</u> Production #: <u>1042</u>
MUSIC SPOTTING NOTES

REEL 1   (28 Starts)

1m1a	1:58.92	"Main Title/Theme"
c1:00:00:00		CREDITS INTERCUT WITH AERIAL WS OF ESTATES, BEACH., UPSCALE
c1:01:58:24		PACIFIC COAST EXTERIORS BUILDS TO MAIN TITLE, HUGE ESTATE,
Background Instrumental		SULTRY BEDROOM SCENE WITH BLONDE AND DELANEY [BLACK 01:55:08-01] [MUSIC: sexy, suspenseful, fatalistic, foreboding, relentless.]

1m2   1:50.51   "Candlestick Killing"
   c1:04:32:03   EXT WS OF DARK CLIFF TO BLONDE LEAVING DELANEY IN BED. CUTS
   c1:06:22:15   TO WHITE BCH HOUSE.   LISA WAKES, CHECKS TIME, BYE TO
   Background Instrumental   SLEEPING JAKE. CUT TO DELANEY GOES TO BALCONY, MOON & CLIFF
                                SHOTS. TEMPO INCREASES AS CANDLESTICK LIFTED, SHE MOVES
                                TOWARD DELANEY, STRIKES REPEATEDLY, HE CLINGS TO RAILING,
                                SHE POUNDS FINGERS 'TIL HE PLUNGES DOWN CLIFF. [MUSIC: LISA-same
                                sultry, starts off a little sad. Danger, small element of horror.]

1m4a   57.69   "Looking For Keys"
   c1:07:26:00   JAKE LOOKS FOR KEYS AS CORY HOVERS, HE FINDS THEM, KISS, DIAL.
   c1:08:23:19   JAKE LEAVES, EXT DECK, SHE SHUTS DOOR. [MUSIC: little sensitive and
   Background Instrumental   sad]

1m4c   3:08.12   "Airport Sting"
   c1:09:16:19   LITTLE BANGS UP AGAINST CAR SUDDENLY. DET.S BANTER ABOUT $,
   c1:12:24:17   TRUST, ARREST. LYLE LEAVES. PLANE LS, JAKE AND LITTLE MEET
   Background Instrumental   GOBO & THUGS. FIGHT BETWEEN THUGS AND LITTLE. JAKE
                                INTERVENES, LITTLE RUNS OFF AS THEY SLUG JAKE, DISCOVER HE'S
                                PACKING. THUGS SHOOT AFTER JAKE AS GOBO YELLS AND GETS IN
                                LIMO, THUGS RETURN AND DRIVE OFF. HIGH ENERGY, MUSIC TAILS
                                OUT OVER HAZY WS OF HUGE PLANE. [MUSIC: danger, industrial,
                                forboding, brass/perc. lots]

1m6a   1:24.02   "Beached Body"
   c1:13:42:17   EXT MS BCH LYLE/JAKE CONT. CONVERSATION ABOUT TIM'S DATE AS
   c1:15:06:15   THEY WALK TO WATER. CORONOR COMMENTS ON POSSIBLE
   Background Instrumental   CONDITION OF DEATH. DET.S WALK AWAY AND DECIDE TO
                                INVESTIGATE HOUSE. EOR. [MUSIC: POV Cory-comtemplative, concerned.
                                Harp plucking, string pad.]

Page 1

spotting notes prepared by Christine Luethje

Sample Spotting Notes #3 (notes entered into a spreadsheet program)

RUNNING HARD - SPOTTING NOTES

NO.	TITLE	TYPE	LENGTH	IN/OUT	SMPTE	CUE PARAMETER DETAILS	SCENE DESCRIPTION AND MUSIC NOTES	OTHER NOTES
1M1	MAIN TITLE	SONG	0:00:26	IN	01:00:00:00	IN: In at Top		
				OUT	01:00:25:26	OUT: Tails out over CUT		
1M2	GHARRETT'S STORY	SONG	0:01:06	IN	01:02:30:00	IN: PRELAP CUT to SIDE Gharrett INT car driving	DESCRIPTION: Jenny narrates loss of Gharrett's mom, grave site	
				OUT	01:03:35:25	OUT: Tails out over CUT	MUSIC: Joni Mitchell-ish, pop/folk ballad, F vocal, Gtr.	
1M3	THE SHOWCASE	SONG	0:01:05	IN	01:03:47:20	IN: After CUT to leering bar owner holding mic	DESCRIPTION: Jenny starts to sing to rowdy audience, they slowly begin to listen	
				OUT	01:04:52:19	OUT: Out on car door slam by Gharrett	MUSIC: Jenny sings, Joni Mitchell-ish, pop/folk ballad, F vocal, Gtr.	
1M4	FRIENDS APPROACH CAR	SCORE	0:00:18	IN	01:05:00:07	IN: CUT SIDE Gharrett notices approach in s.v. mirror	DESCRIPTION: Gharrett notice two people approaching and get gun out only to realize they are his friends	HIT GUN, BUT NOT TOO HARD
				OUT	01:05:18:02	OUT: Tails before cut to friends	MUSIC: Dark tension, Strgs., then tinkling innocent, foreboding Pno on gun, industrial sting (cym) on friends	
1M5	SCORE ON THIS	SONG	0:00:40	IN	01:05:20:03	IN: LS friends at car	DESCRIPTION: Chad pulls out a joint and they smoke it	
				OUT	01:06:00:14	OUT: CUT to back of Jenny on stage	MUSIC: Lenny Kravitz-ish, hip hop groove, alternative compress R&B vocal.	
1M6	SHOWCASE CONTINUES	SONG	0:00:14	IN	01:06:00:14	IN: CU Jenny	DESCRIPTION: Back to Jenny wooing audience	CONTINUATION OF 1M3?
				OUT	01:06:14:13	OUT: Tails out by CUT Leering owner's approach		
1M7	GETTING HIGH	SONG	0:00:48	IN	01:06:26:06	IN: CUT SIDE Gharrett smoking joint	DESCRIPTION: Boys smoke joint	
				OUT	01:07:14:20	OUT: By CUT to Dix' back as he approaches their car		
1M8	DIX SNIFFS/BUST	SCORE	0:02:47	IN	01:07:19:23	IN: CUT to Gharrett after Dix DIAL. "...fast."	DESCRIPTION: Smoking interrupted by Officer Dix approach & harassment	LOW STRINGS + PERCUSSION
				OUT	01:10:06:24	OUT: MUSIC PAUSES as Dix holds up cocaine	MUSIC: Pulsing, Strgs., Hm hold, Tension, builds to cocaine reveal	
1M9	TROY GETS IT	SCORE	0:03:19	IN	01:10:07:03	IN: Dead Troy on ground as DIX foot kicks him	DESCRIPTION: Chad and Gharrett shocked then boys fight cops. Chad dies as Gharrett drives off and Dix chases.	START CHASE ON CAR DRIVE OFF
				OUT	01:13:26:13	OUT: CUT to Sierra Bar/Diner	MUSIC: Fast tempo, driving, lots of percussion, industrial fighting music, Tpts., hits	
1M10	PUNCHING THE OWNER/ESCAPE	SCORE	0:01:46	IN	01:14:30:28	IN: Jenny punches owner	DESCRIPTION: Jenny punches owner and flees to find and help Gharrett escape Dix.	
				OUT	01:15:26:06	OUT: Music changes on CUT to LS couple running		

Running Hard Page 1

MASTER CUE LIST

Prepared By   Music Editor

Users   Music Editor, Composer, Director

Maintained   In main work file for project. Copies to music editor and director

Description   This is a summary of the Spotting Notes, and serves as a summary of all the cues that are to be written for a project. This document is the basis for creating the Master Cue List Worksheet presented later in this section.

A copy of the Master Cue List should <u>always</u> be given to the filmmaker, as it will serve as a point of reference in future discussions regarding cues, duration, style, and other musical details.

Sample Master Cue List #1

"MALIBU NIGHTS"
MASTER CUE LIST

CUE	TITLE	TYPE/USAGE	TIME
1m1a	Main Title	SCORE/DRAMA	1:59
1m1b	Love/Rocks	SONG/SEXY	1:15
1m2	Candlestick Killing	SCORE/DRAMA	1:50
1m3	Morning Jake	SCORE/MOOD	0:32
1m4a	Looking for Keys	SCORE/MOOD	1:01
1m4b	Legit Love at Airport	SCORE/DRAMA	0:50
1m4c	Airport Sting	SCORE/ACTION	3:10
1m5	Gotta Go Back	SCORE/DRAMA	0:19
1m6a	Beached Body	SCORE/MOOD	1:32
1m6b	House Investigation	SCORE/DRAMA	2:05
1m7	Family Investigation	SCORE/DRAMA	3:35
1m8	Meet Me In The Hall	SCORE/SEXY	2:37
1m9	Been In Records	SCORE/MOOD	0:35
1m10a	Check Out the Lady	SCORE/DRAMA	5:40
1m10b	Tim Questions Jake	SCORE/DRAMA	0:47
1m11	Coroner Says Murder	SCORE/DRAMA	2:56
1m12	A Little Chase	SCORE/ACTION	4:51
1m13a	Elaine's House	SCORE/DRAMA	4:35
1m13b	Hey, Baby	SCORE/MOOD	0:51
1m14	A Little Murder	SCORE/DRAMA	3:21
1m15	Real Estate Questions	SCORE/MOOD	1:55
1m16a	Jake Chases Lisa	SCORE/ACTION	2:33
1m16b	A Little Discovery	SCORE/DRAMA	1:36
1m17a	Where's Jake?	SCORE/DRAMA	0:20
1m17b	A Little Dead	SCORE/DRAMA	0:30
1m18a	Jake Comforts Lisa	SCORE/DRAMA	2:45
1m18b	Second Thoughts	SCORE/DRAMA	0:40
1m18c	Lisa Escapes	SCORE/ACTION	0:40
1m19	Property Info/Cops Fight	SCORE/ACTION	3:54
1m20	Bit Into the Apple	SCORE/DRAMA	3:57
1m21	Lisa Visits Lyle	SCORE/DRAMA	3:02
1m22	You Seem Distant	SCORE/DRAMA	0:57
1m23a	Lisa Wants Out	SCORE/DRAMA	0:39
1m23b	End Chase	SCORE/ACTION	5:01
1m23c	Jake to the Rescue	SCORE/ACTION	3:52
1m24	On the Rocks	SCORE/DRAMA	3:20
1m25	End Credits	SCORE/DRAMA	3:02
		TOTAL MUSIC:	**83:04**

Sample Master Cue List #2 (divided into score and song cues)

RUNNING HARD - MASTER CUE LIST

	CUE	TITLE	SMPTE IN	SMPTE OUT	LENGTH
	1M4	FRIENDS APPROACH CAR	01:05:00:07	01:05:18:02	0:00:18
	1M8	DIX SNIFFS/BUST	01:07:19:23	01:10:06:24	0:02:47
	1M9	TROY GETS IT	01:10:07:03	01:13:26:13	0:03:19
	1M10	PUNCHING THE OWNER/ESCAPE	01:14:30:28	01:15:26:06	0:01:46
	1M13	ROUTE 395	01:21:50:18	01:22:10:29	0:00:20
	1M16	LONG WAY DOWN	01:25:47:04	01:26:43:21	0:00:57
S	1M18	ARE WE LOOKING FOR DIX?	01:28:25:08	01:28:47:25	0:00:23
	1M22	GOOD FOOD	01:32:25:19	01:34:13:09	0:01:48
C	1M23	BACK @ THE STATION	01:34:13:10	01:34:46:01	0:00:33
	1M24	CAN'T PAY	01:35:44:11	01:37:27:00	0:01:43
O	1M25	BRING THEM IN ALIVE	01:37:33:12	01:38:05:24	0:00:38
	1M27	INT HOTEL/TV NEWS	01:43:01:10	01:43:08:15	0:00:07
R	1M28	HOTEL ROOM	01:43:08:13	01:45:19:27	0:02:11
	1M30	PLEASE! (GRAMPS)	01:45:26:01	01:46:20:24	0:00:55
E	1M31	DIX WAITS	01:46:32:00	01:47:48:14	0:01:16
	1M32	BEAUTIFUL CANYONS	01:47:48:15	01:48:21:11	0:00:33
	1M33	DIX PARKS	01:48:21:12	01:48:30:13	0:00:09
	1M34	SUNSET LOVE	01:48:30:14	01:50:17:02	0:01:47
C	1M35	DIX DREAM/TRUCK	01:50:17:03	01:51:38:04	0:01:21
	1M38	MARRY ME	01:53:38:16	01:56:56:20	0:03:18
U	1M39	TRAIN/DIX DRIVING	01:56:56:20	01:59:31:14	0:02:35
	1M44	HANK VISITS TOMMY	02:08:11:11	02:11:35:26	0:02:21
E	1M45	GOTTA GET OUTTA HERE	02:11:42:00	02:13:24:13	0:01:42
	1M46	HANK SQUEALS	02:13:24:13	02:14:47:02	0:01:23
S	1M47	ID POSITIVE	02:14:47:02	02:15:18:26	0:00:32
	1M48	I WANTED THIS KID	02:15:18:26	02:17:50:07	0:02:31
	1M49	DIX IS COMING/FIGHT TO DEATH	02:17:50:08	02:21:11:17	0:03:21
	1M50	FLYING FALL	02:21:11:17	02:21:43:08	0:00:32
	1M51	HE'S ONE OF MINE/TOMMY'S REVENGE	02:21:43:08	02:22:39:15	0:00:56
	1M52	TOMMY'S DEPARTURE/OUT OF WATER	02:22:47:08	02:23:51:11	0:01:04
	1M54	GHARRETT LIVES ON/END CREDITS	02:24:51:10	02:27:18:29	0:02:28

	CUE	TITLE	SMPTE IN	SMPTE OUT	LENGTH
	1M1	MAIN TITLE	01:00:00:00	01:00:25:26	0:00:26
	1M2	GHARRETT'S STORY	01:02:30:00	01:03:35:25	0:01:06
	1M3	THE SHOWCASE	01:03:47:20	01:04:52:19	0:01:05
S	1M5	SCORE ON THIS	01:05:20:03	01:06:00:14	0:00:40
	1M6	SHOWCASE CONTINUES	01:06:00:14	01:06:14:13	0:00:14
O	1M7	GETTING HIGH	01:06:26:06	01:07:14:20	0:00:48
	1M11	FRAN'S	01:19:54:20	01:20:15:06	0:00:21
N	1M12	I'M GOING WITH YOU	01:20:41:05	01:21:28:08	0:00:47
	1M14	ESCAPE ROUTE	01:22:11:00	01:23:49:17	0:01:39
G	1M15	HWY CHASE	01:22:49:18	01:25:47:03	0:01:00
	1M17	WATCH THE ROCKS	01:26:43:22	01:28:22:18	0:01:39
	1M19	OUT OF GAS	01:28:57:20	01:31:34:26	0:02:37
	1M20	DON'T WANT TO TALK	01:31:33:25	01:31:49:11	0:00:16
C	1M21	WINDMILLS	01:32:02:27	01:32:25:18	0:00:23
	1M26	GUITAR DOODLING	01:40:08:10	01:40:45:20	0:00:37
U	1M29	OLD MAN/GETAWAY	01:45:19:28	01:46:33:16	0:01:14
	1M36	DID HE HAVE A GUN?	01:51:38:05	01:51:49:02	0:00:11
E	1M37	I'M PREGNANT	01:51:52:03	01:53:38:15	0:01:46
	1M40	INTRO TO DAD/CHECKS ID	01:59:33:11	01:59:49:14	0:00:13
S	1M41	ARE YOU GOOD PEOPLE?	02:01:20:16	02:01:57:10	0:00:37
	1M42	SHE DIED?	02:03:00:21	02:03:49:16	0:00:49
	1M43	TIME TO CRY	02:06:26:20:	02:06:50:06	0:00:24
	1M53	JENNY'S STORY	02:23:44:21	02:24:00:00	0:00:15

TOTAL SCORE		0:45:34
TOTAL SONGS		0:19:07
TOTAL MUSIC		1:04:41

BREAKDOWN NOTES

Prepared By   Music Editor

Users   Music Editor, Composer

Maintained   In main work file for project. Copy to music editor

Description   A complete breakdown of the entire scene to be scored, including the timings and descriptions of action events, important *hit* locations, important dialog lines, cuts and camera moves, and the beginning and ending times of music cues.

Depending on the type of project and budget constraints, you may want to ask the music editor to produce more or less detailed breakdown notes. One way to reduce music editor costs is to ask the music editor to provide only the major camera changes and action events of a scene and avoid references to dialogue or minor action elements.

Sample Breakdown Notes (less detailed format)

relative time from the beginning of the cue

refers to the type of time code

Production: **MALIBU NIGHTS**   Production #: **1042**

Cue: **1m21** "**Lisa Visits Lyle's**"

Begins at **c2:08:29:06** in Reel/Act 1

ABS. SMPTE #(29):	REL. TIME:		
c2:08:29:06	0.00	CUT	Start of Cue. LS EXT Lyle's house.
c2:08:31:23	2.57	CUT	MS pan up to Lisa walking up stairs. CONT. knocking on sliding glass door.
c2:08:46:05	16.98	CUT	INT house as Lyle comes to door. CONT. "**Hi.**"
c2:08:50:17	21.39	CUT	CU EXT LISA takes off sunglasses "**Can I come in.**" CONT. LYLE "**Sure.**" She enters and they talk.
c2:08:57:00	27.83		LISA "**So what's going on Lyle?**"
c2:09:00:00	30.83	CUT	"**Is Elaine trying to kill me now?**" DIAL: CONT. LYLE "**I'll call.**" LISA "**No!**" CONT.
c2:09:43:21	1:14.57		Lisa grabs the phone.
c2:09:53:06	1:24.08		Lyle makes pass at Lisa and she rejects him. CONT.
c2:10:07:28	1:38.83	CUT	SLAP! Lisa slaps Lyle. She gets up. CONT. DIAL: Lyle's sorry, broke, water.
c2:10:50:04	2:21.07	CUT	MS CU Lyle in bathroom calls Elaine.
c2:11:02:12	2:33.35	CUT	WS EXT Elaine's house.
c2:11:04:17	2:35.52	CUT	INT Elaine picks up phone "**Yeah.**" CONT. She tells Lyle to keep her there.
c2:11:12:01	2:43.00	CUT	Lyle.
c2:11:13:06	2:44.16	CUT	Elaine.
c2:11:16:11	2:47.33	CUT	Lyle.
c2:11:18:01	2:49.00	CUT	CU Elaine "**Should be quick.**" She gets up and leaves room.
c2:11:28:04	2:59.11	CUT	Lyle hangs up.
c2:11:34:09	3:05.29	CUT	Lisa lies down.
c2:11:39:28	3:10.92	CUT	EXT DAY Police dept.
c2:11:45:09	3:16.30	CUT	INT JAKE and TIM talk about Elaine.

Malibu Nights 1m21 page 1

breakdown notes prepared by Christine Luethje

c2:11:54:00	3:25.01		BEEP! Tim checks pager "**Shit, my ex-wife. I'll meet up with you later.**" "**Alright.**" They part.
c2:11:59:20	3:30.68	CUT	Tim EXT walking.
c2:12:03:15	3:34.51	CUT	INT Lyle's place, Lisa asleep.
c2:12:07:04	3:38.15	CUT	Tim gets out of car, DIAL: Lyle about Lisa, ascend stairs.
c2:12:27:20	3:58.71		Tim grabs Lisa's hand and turns her, cuffing her. She protests.
c2:12:30:14	4:01.51	CUT	LYLE "**I'm sorry. He came in.** " LISA "**Bullshit.**" "**....weird, babe.**"
c2:12:40:10	4:11.38	CUT	TIM meanly to Lisa "**Elaine wants to see you.**" "**You're lying.**"
c2:12:42:12	4:13.45	CUT	TIM "**I can put you out! Or you can be cool.**"
c2:12:45:28	4:16.99	CUT	LISA "**ALRIGHT! ...**" TIM "**..the door.**"
c2:12:51:18	4:22.66	CUT	CU EXT car wheels peel out.
c2:12:54:16	4:25.60	CUT	End of Cue. EOR.

TOTAL TIME - 4:25.60

END CUE 1m21

Malibu Nights 1m21 page 2

MASTER CUE LIST WORKSHEET

Prepared By   Music Editor or Composer

Users   Composer, Music Editor

Maintained   In main work file for project. Copy for music editor

Description   This document is designed to be a scorecard for tracking the writing progress of each music cue. Each cue's vital information is listed, and the composer can mark each cue as it is completed.

This document also allows the composer to see where each cue lies in relation to the cues before and after it. Timing and stylistic considerations can be planned using this document as a road map of the project.

You may want to consider keeping this document in computerized form and updating it regularly as cues are completed. Changes in start and end times, cue titles, and other details can be noted on this document and entered into a master version on computer for update purposes.

Sample Master Cue List Worksheet

DIAMONDS IN THE ROUGH MASTER CUE LIST WORKSHEET

	CUE	TITLE	TIME	CURRENT SMPTE		NEW SMPTE		TYPE	THEME	WHO	PROGRESS				NOTES
				IN	OUT	IN	OUT				WRITE	FIX	REWRITE	APPROVE	
1	1m2	Blythe Delivery	2:14	1:02:51:00	1:05:05:10			Synth	Malcolm	Mark	✓	☒	☒	✓	
2	1m4	Gina's Theme	5:57	1:05:42:20	1:11:39:28			Live	Gina	Lisa	✓	✓	✓	✓	
3	1m5	Simon's Chase	4:03	1:11:44:01	1:15:46:25			Live	Simon	Mark	✓	☒	☒	✓	Let end ring long
4	1m6	Catch a Cab	:36	1:15:50:11	1:16:29:06	1:15:55:11	1:16:38:06	Synth	Running	Mark	✓	✓	☒	✓	
5	1m9	Diamond Salute #1	:21	1:19:51:11	1:20:12:12			Live	Diamond	Lisa	✓	☒	☒	✓	
6	1m11	Bad Cop	2:03	1:21:28:06	1:23:31:26			Synth	Bad Cop	Mark	✓	☒	☒	✓	
7	1m13	Simon is Alive	:20	1:24:30:21	1:24:50:27			Edit	Simon	Mark	☒	☒	☒	✓	EDIT after mix
8	1m14	Three in a Taxi	1:36	1:24:50:28	1:26:26:18			Synth	Running	Mark	✓	☒	☒	✓	
9	1m15	Bad-Cop Chase	2:55	1:26:26:19	1:29:21:27			Live	Bad Cop	Mark	✓	☒	☒	✓	
10	1m16	Taxi Blowup	:56	1:29:57:14	1:30:53:24			Synth	Running	Mark	✓	✓	☒	✓	
11	1m17	Diamond Salute #2	:25	1:30:54:10	1:31:25:10			Live	Diamond	Lisa	✓	✓	☒	✓	
12	1m18	Scheming about cop	2:15	1:31:25:10	1:33:12:15		1:33:00:00	Synth	Running	Mark	✓	✓	☒	✓	
13	1m20	Embarrassed Cop	2:36	1:34:51:02	1:37:29:17			Synth	Bad Cop	Mark	✓	☒	✓	✓	
14	1m21	Gina Escapes	:30	1:38:02:18	1:38:35:06			Synth	Gina	Lisa	✓	☒	✓	✓	
15	1m22	Maria's theme	3:00	1:38:48:00	1:41:48:00			Live	Maria	Lisa	✓	☒	☒	✓	
16	1m23	Diamond Salute #3	:54	1:42:05:03	1:43:02:07	1:41:58:12		Live	Diamond	Lisa	✓	✓	☒	✓	
17	1m24	Cop Checkout	1:12	1:43:31:06	1:44:43:23			Synth	Maria	Lisa	✓	☒	✓	✓	
18	1m25	Maria Makes a Deal	1:10	1:45:28:00	1:45:54:19			Synth	Maria	Lisa	✓	☒	✓	✓	
19	1m26	Anthony's Theme	1:18	1:47:56:27	1:49:20:14			Synth	Anthony	Mark	✓	☒	☒	✓	
20	1m27	Sleepytime	2:31	1:50:19:21	1:52:50:25			Live	Lover	Mark	✓	☒	☒	✓	
21	1m30	Gina Sneaks Out	3:24	1:56:43:09	2:00:07:02			Edit	Gina	Lisa	☒	☒	☒	✓	EDIT after mix
22	1m31	Cat Fight / Help Cop	3:43	2:00:42:05	2:04:24:23			Edit	Maria	Lisa	☒	☒	☒	✓	EDIT after mix
23	1m35	Eric Makes a Call	:23	2:09:41:01	2:10:07:13			Synth	Malcolm	Mark	✓	✓	✓	✓	
24	1m36	Shipyard	4:45	2:10:29:27	2:15:16:14			Synth	Shipyard	Mark	✓	✓	✓	✓	
25	1m37	Diamond Salute #4	:16	2:15:16:06	2:15:34:00	2:15:20:04		Live	Diamond	Lisa	✓	✓	☒	✓	
26	1m38	Bad Cop Returns	1:27	2:15:32:11	2:16:59:17			Synth	Bad Cop	Mark	✓	☒	☒	✓	
27	1m39	Malcolm Arrives	4:30	2:16:59:18	2:21:29:28			Live	Malcolm	Lisa	✓	☒	☒	✓	
28	1m40	Fight for the Diamonds	1:28	2:21:42:20	2:23:10:06			Synth	Dixieland	Mark	✓	☒	☒	✓	
29	1m41	Into the Sunset	2:11	2:23:21:13	2:25:32:00			Live	Sunset	Lisa	✓	✓	☒	✓	

RECORDING SCHEDULE

Prepared By   Composer, Contractor, or Composer's Assistant

Users   Everyone involved with the recording session (musicians, engineer, composer, music editor, assistants, etc.)

Maintained   In main work file for project. Copies to all as necessary.

Description   Informs everyone of the time and place for each recording session. It may also include information about the instrumentation and any special notes (where to park, etc.). It should also include any appropriate contact numbers, and if necessary, a map.

The recording schedule should be sent or faxed to all parties involved in the recording session, including the composer's team (music editor, contractor, orchestrator, copyist), the musicians, engineer, and any appropriate people on the client team (director, post production personnel, producers, executives). Although the schedule may only repeat what was said in a phone call, we've found that providing it in writing is always appreciated.

Depending on whether your recording session is union or non-union, you may want to carefully plan how much music you will be able to record per hour. Also note that it is customary to give musicians a 10 minute break each hour.

Sample Recording Schedule

"MALIBU NIGHTS"
RECORDING SCHEDULE
CINEMATRAX STUDIOS

CONTACT: Mark Northam 1-888-SCORE-38

MONDAY, JUNE 17
Call Times:

	Engineer	8:30am
	Assistant	8:30am

All STRINGS   9:00am - 12:00pm
1:00pm - 4:00pm
4:00-5:00 HOLD for overtime if necessary

TUESDAY, JUNE 18
Call Times:

	Engineer	9:30am
	Assistant	9:45am

HARP   10:00am - 12:30pm
ALL BRASS   2:00pm - 5:00pm
5:00 - 6:00pm HOLD for overtime if necessary

WEDNESDAY, JUNE 19
Mixing Sessions   9:00am - 1:00pm
1:45pm - 7:00pm

THURSDAY, JUNE 20
Mixing Sessions   9:00am - 1:00pm
1:45pm - 5:00pm
Make Backups   (evening)

FRIDAY, JUNE 21
DELIVER MIXDOWN TAPES WITH DOCUMENTATION TO CLIENT - 10:00AM

1146 N. Central Ave. #103 ✦ GLENDALE, CALIFORNIA 91202
TELEPHONE: 1-888-SCORE-38 ✦ INTERNET: www.cinematrax.com

SESSION CHECKLIST

Prepared By   Composer, Composer's Assistant

Users   Composer, Engineer, Composer's Assistant

Maintained   In main work file for project. Copies for music editor and engineer

Description   This is a handy checklist to complete before each recording session. It can help remind you of things that need to be done in preparation for a session (tape formatting, equipment rentals, etc.) and can make the difference between a satisfactory session and a great one. We use this checklist at our home studio and when we use outside studios for bigger orchestras.

Sample Session Checklist

CINEMATRAX SESSION CHECKLIST

Session: _DIAMONDS_   Contact: _MARK NORTHAM_

Location: _CINEMATRAX_   Phone: _(888) 726-7338_

Date: _1|1|97_   Time: _9:00 am_

✓   Set aside all blank tapes required:

DA-88: Length: _3_   Qty: _120_

DAT: Length: _4_   Qty: _120_

Format DAT at: _X_ 44.1K   _____ 48K

VIDEO: Length: _____   Qty: _____

✓   Format and Stripe DA-88 Tape(s)

Instructions: _STRIPE ALL DA-88 TAPES @ 44.1K._
START TC AT 0:58:00:00, STRIPE ENTIRE TAPES

✓   Rent all equipment necessary

Instructions: _2 DA-88's WITH 1/4" TRS_
SNAKES. RENT FOR MON-FRI.

✓   Check Inventory of Food/Drinks:

✓ Water (individual bottles)   ✓ Purchase Food (onsite session)
✓ Coca-Cola   _WILL ORDER LUNCH_
✓ Diet Coke   _FOR DELIVERY_
✓ Snapple Drinks
✓ Coffee
✓ Snacks

✓   Confirm Musicians and Engineer - date and time info

_N/A_   Confirm Outside Studio: _____

_____   Other: _____

RECORDING SESSION CUE WORKSHEET

Prepared By   Music Editor, Composer, or Composer's Assistant

Users   Composer, Music Editor, Engineer, Copyist

Maintained   In main work file for project. Copies for music editor, copyist and engineer

Description   We use this document constantly during recording sessions to track the progress of the session, to inform the engineer about what cues and instruments need to be recorded, and generally to keep track of the music to make sure we don't miss any details of a cue in the hectic environment of a recording session.

This worksheet is based on the Master Cue List Worksheet and includes details available after each cue has been composed. Information in this worksheet includes instrumentation, final timings, chart preparation information, mix information, and final tape information including which final mix tape contains each cue and which tracks on the tape were used.

Prior to the recording session, this worksheet is given to the copyist along with a recording schedule so he/she can plan his work efforts. Typically, the copyist works on a very tight schedule, sometimes working right up to the last minute before a session.

Sample Recording Session Cue List Worksheet

DIAMONDS IN THE ROUGH RECORDING SESSION CUE LIST WORKSHEET

	CUE	TITLE	TIME	IN	OUT	INSTRUMENTS			CHTS.	REC.	MIX	DA-88	NOTES
						Strings	Brass	Woodwinds					
1	1m2	Blythe Delivery	2:14	1:02:51:00	1:05:05:10								
2	1m4	Gina's Theme	5:57	1:05:42:20	1:11:39:28	Vln, Vc		Pic, Fl, Cl, B. Cl	✓				
3	1m5	Simon's Chase	4:03	1:11:44:01	1:15:46:25		Tpt, Tbn	Pic, Fl, Cl, B. Cl	✓				SEPARATE RHYTHM TRACKS
4	1m6	Catch a Cab	:36	1:15:50:11	1:16:29:06								
5	1m9	Diamond Salute #1	:21	1:19:51:11	1:20:12:12		Tpt, Tbn		✓				
6	1m11	Bad Cop	2:03	1:21:28:06	1:23:31:26								
7	1m13	Simon is Alive	:20	1:24:30:21	1:24:50:27								
8	1m14	Three in a Taxi	1:36	1:24:50:28	1:26:26:18								Xfade to m15
9	1m15	Bad-Cop Chase	2:55	1:26:26:19	1:29:21:27		Tpt, Tbn		✓				
10	1m16	Taxi Blowup	:56	1:29:57:14	1:30:53:24								
11	1m17	Diamond Salute #2	:25	1:30:54:10	1:31:25:10		Tpt, Tbn		✓				
12	1m18	Scheming about cop	2:15	1:31:25:10	1:33:12:15								
13	1m20	Embarrassed Cop	2:36	1:34:51:02	1:37:29:17								
14	1m21	Gina Escapes	:30	1:38:02:18	1:38:35:06								
15	1m22	Maria's theme	3:00	1:38:48:00	1:41:48:00	Vln, Vc			✓	✓			
16	1m23	Diamond Salute #3	:54	1:42:05:03	1:43:02:07		Tpt, Tbn		✓	✓			
17	1m24	Cop Checkout	1:12	1:43:31:06	1:44:43:23								
18	1m25	Maria Makes a Deal	1:10	1:45:28:00	1:45:54:19								
19	1m26	Anthony's Theme	1:18	1:47:56:27	1:49:20:14								
20	1m27	Sleepytime	2:31	1:50:19:21	1:52:50:25		Tbn		✓				
21	1m30	Gina Sneaks Out	3:24	1:56:43:09	2:00:07:02								
22	1m31	Cat Fight / Help Cop	3:43	2:00:42:05	2:04:24:23								
23	1m35	Eric Makes a Call	:23	2:09:41:01	2:10:07:13								
24	1m36	Shipyard	4:45	2:10:29:27	2:15:16:14								
25	1m37	Diamond Salute #4	:16	2:15:16:06	2:15:34:00		Tpt, Tbn		✓	✓			
26	1m38	Bad Cop Returns	1:27	2:15:32:11	2:16:59:17								
27	1m39	Malcolm Arrives	4:30	2:16:59:18	2:21:29:28		Tpt, Tbn		✓	✓			
28	1m40	Fight for the Diamonds	1:28	2:21:42:20	2:23:10:06								
29	1m41	Into the Sunset	2:11	2:23:21:13	2:25:32:00	Vln, Vc		Fl, Ob, Cl	✓	✓			

RECORDING SESSION ORDER

Prepared By   Music Editor, Composer, or Composer's Assistant

Users   Composer, Music Editor, Engineer, Musicians

Maintained   In main work file for project. Copies for music editor and engineer

Description   This document is used for planning a recording session. After the music has been composed and the copyist is working on creating parts for the musicians, the composer can plan the order of cues to be recorded at the session.

Since time is valuable at recording sessions, it's always best to do as much planning as possible to help the session run smoothly. It's a good idea to prioritize your cues and establish a preferred recording order. Among the factors you should consider about each cue when establishing the order are:

- What are the most important cues to be recorded. You may want to place these cues near the beginning of the session.

- Try to group cues of a similar style together. Cues that use the same musical material should usually be recorded close together so the musicians can move quickly through them as they become familiar with the music.

- Are there any cues that are particularly difficult for the musicians? Try and spread these cues out and schedule them after breaks when the musicians are rested.

- Can the director only attend part of the recording session? If so, you may want to determine which cues it would be important for him/her to be present for so you can schedule them accordingly. Cues that involve improvisation by the musicians are often good candidates for director input and approval at the recording session.

Sample Recording Session Order

DIAMONDS IN THE ROUGH

RECORDING ORDER

SESSION #		CUE	TITLE	LENGTH	INSTRUMENTS		
					Strings	Brass	Woodwinds
Session #1	1	1m9	Diamond Salute #1	:21		Tpt, Tbn	
Brass	2	1m17	Diamond Salute #2	:25		Tpt, Tbn	
9am-2pm	3	1m23	Diamond Salute #3	:54		Tpt, Tbn	
	4	1m37	Diamond Salute #4	:16		Tpt, Tbn	
	5	1m5	Simon's Chase	4:03		Tpt, Tbn	
	6	1m15	Bad-Cop Chase	2:55		Tpt, Tbn	
	7	1m39	Malcolm Arrives	4:30		Tpt, Tbn	
	8	1m27	Sleepytime	2:31		Tbn	
Session #2	9	1m22	Maria's theme	3:00	Vln, Vc		
Strings &	10	1m4	Gina's Theme	5:57	Vln, Vc		Pic, Fl, Cl, B. Cl
Woodwinds	11	1m41	Into the Sunset	2:11	Vln, Vc		Fl, Ob, Cl
3pm-7pm	12	1m5	Simon's Chase	4:03			Pic, Fl, Cl, B. Cl

TRACK SHEET

Prepared By   Engineer (usually) or Composer

Users   Engineer, Composer, Post Production Facility

Maintained   Along with all copies of master tapes. Copies to post production facility for reference during prelay and the dubbing sessions.

Description   If you do recording projects using tape formats with more than two tracks (such as Tascam DA-88, Alesis ADAT, analog 2-inch 24 track), track sheets are absolutely necessary. They should present the vital information about what's on the tape in an easy-to-read format.

Track sheets often serve two main purposes:

1.   To maintain a complete record of what music and instruments are recorded on each track of your tape.

2.   To maintain an accurate record of the time code information for each cue, including the time code start location and type (drop frame, non-drop, or other) of time code used on the tape.

Some composers keep the track sheets bundled with the tape itself, and others keep a library or binder containing all their track sheets (often sorted alphabetically by project). In either case, track sheets are one of the most important documents in your studio, as they contain all the vital information about your multitrack tapes.

Sample Track Sheet

CINEMATRAX 1-888-SCORE-38

PROJECT: DIAMONDS IN THE ROUGH
CUE / SONG TITLE: 1M5 | SIMON'S CHASE

CLIENT: ROJAK
PRODUCTION NO.:

COMPOSER: NORTHAM/MILLER
ENGINEER: M. STERN

DATE: 1/1/97

1 TRUMPET	2 TROMBONE	3 COMBINED BRASS (DOUBLE)	4 PICCOLO	5 FLUTE	6 CLARINET	7 BASS CLARINET	8
9	10	11	12	13	14	15	16
17	18	19	20	21	22	23	24

NOTES: SEPARATE SYNTH RHYTHM TRACKS ON MIXDOWN FOR SURROUND CHANNELS

TIMECODE TYPE
☒ 29.97 Non-Drop
☐ Drop frame
☐ Other: ____

	Hour	Minute	Second	Frame
AUDIO TIME CODE START:	1	11	44	01
VIDEO TIME CODE START:				
TIME CODE OFFSET:				

PERFORMING RIGHTS CUE SHEET

Prepared By   Music Editor or Composer

Users   Composer, Music Editor, Performing Rights Organization(s), Film Production Company

Maintained   In main work file for project. Copies to music editor, film production company, and all performing rights organization(s) listed on cues.

Description   This is a vital document you should pay careful attention to for each project. It contains specific information about each cue and overall project information that the performing rights organizations (PROs) require in order to collect domestic and foreign performing rights royalties for you. The cue sheet for each project should be sent to all of the PROs (ASCAP, BMI, SESAC) that are listed on the cue sheet.

Each Performing Rights Cue Sheet should contain the following information:

- The title of the project and film production company

- Key personnel, including the director, producer(s), and key actors (the ones starring in the project)

- The country of origin and release date for the project (in television, the first air date)

- The type of initial release (theatrical, video, other)

- For each cue, the following should be listed:

  1. **Title** of the cue (and *M number* if possible)

  2. **Composer(s)** and their percentage split(s) (this will determine the split of the writer performing rights royalties)

3. **Publisher(s)** and their percentage split(s) (this will determine the split of the publisher performing rights royalties)

4. **Affiliation** of both the composer and publisher — which performing rights organization they belong to (BMI, ASCAP, SESAC, etc.)

5. **Usage Category** of the cue, or how it was used. Some examples of cue usage are *Visual Vocal, Visual Instrumental, Background Vocal,* and *Background Instrumental.* You should also note if the cue is being used for any special purpose, such as main title, end title, etc. It is important to make sure these are correct because the usage determines the rate at which the cue will be paid. Check with your performing rights organization for their specific types and codes for usage.

6. **Length** of the cue (as actually used in the film)

Note: It is wise to call the PROs a couple of weeks after you submit the cue sheet to confirm they have received it and that it has been entered it into their computer system.

Sample Performing Rights Cue Sheet

MUSIC CUE SHEET

Project:	**Malibu Nights**		Prepared by:	**Mike Music Editor**
Production Co.:	**FredWorks Films**		Phone**:**	**(310) 555-0000**

9999 Sunset Boulevard
Suite 007
Los Angeles, CA 90099

Executive Producers: **Paul Producer, Pamela Producer**
Principal Actors: **Amy Actress, Adam Actor**
Producer: **Pete Producer**   Director: **Fred Filmmaker**
Country of Origin: **USA**   Date of Release: **April 1, 1997**
First Production: **Video Release**   Date Cue Sheet Prepared: **July 1, 1996**

<u>Cue</u>	<u>Composer(s)</u>	<u>%</u>	<u>Publisher(s)</u>	<u>Affil.</u>	<u>Time</u>
Malibu Nights - M. T. (1m1a)	Mark Northam Lisa Anne Miller	50 50	North Edge Music Miller's Edge Music	ASCAP BMI <u>Main Title</u>	1:59
Elaine's Theme (1m1b)	Mark Northam Lisa Anne Miller	50 50	North Edge Music Miller's Edge Music	ASCAP BMI <u>Background Instrumental</u>	2:40
Candlestick Killing (1m2)	Lisa Anne Miller	100	Miller's Edge Music	BMI <u>Background Instrumental</u>	1:50
Morning Jake (1m3)	Lisa Anne Miller	100	Miller's Edge Music	BMI <u>Background Instrumental</u>	0:32
Looking for the Keys (1m4a)	Mark Northam	100	North Edge Music	ASCAP <u>Background Instrumental</u>	1:01
Airport Sting (1m4c)	Lisa Anne Miller	100	Miller's Edge Music	BMI <u>Background Instrumental</u>	3:10
Beached Body (1m6a)	Mark Northam	100	North Edge Music	ASCAP <u>Background Instrumental</u>	1:32
House Investigation (1m6b)	Lisa Anne Miller	100	Miller's Edge Music	BMI <u>Background Instrumental</u>	2:05
Family Investigation (1m7)	Mark Northam Lisa Anne Miller	50 50	North Edge Music Miller's Edge Music	ASCAP BMI <u>Background Instrumental</u>	3:35
Meet Me In The Hall (1m8)	Mark Northam Lisa Anne Miller	50 50	North Edge Music Miller's Edge Music	ASCAP BMI <u>Background Instrumental</u>	2:37
Check Out The Lady (1m10a)	Lisa Anne Miller	100	Miller's Edge Music	BMI <u>Background Instrumental</u>	5:40

"MALIBU NIGHTS" Cue Sheet - Page 2 of 3

Coroner Says Murder (1m11)	Lisa Anne Miller	100	Miller's Edge Music	BMI	2:56
				Background Instrumental	
A Little Chase (1m12)	Lisa Anne Miller	100	Miller's Edge Music	BMI	4:51
				Background Instrumental	
Elaine's House (1m13a)	Mark Northam	50	North Edge Music	ASCAP	4:35
	Lisa Anne Miller	50	Miller's Edge Music	BMI	
				Background Instrumental	
Hey Baby (1m13b)	Lisa Anne Miller	100	Miller's Edge Music	BMI	0:51
				Background Instrumental	
A Little Murder (1m14)	Mark Northam	100	North Edge Music	ASCAP	3:21
				Background Instrumental	
Real Estate Questions (1m15)	Mark Northam	100	North Edge Music	ASCAP	1:55
				Background Instrumental	
Jake Chases Lisa (1m16a)	Lisa Anne Miller	100	Miller's Edge Music	BMI	2:33
				Background Instrumental	
A Little Discovery (1m16b)	Lisa Anne Miller	100	Miller's Edge Music	BMI	1:36
				Background Instrumental	
A Little Dead (1m17b)	Lisa Anne Miller	100	Miller's Edge Music	BMI	0:30
				Background Instrumental	
Jake Comforts Lisa (1m18a)	Lisa Anne Miller	100	Miller's Edge Music	BMI	2:45
				Background Instrumental	
Lisa Escapes (1m18c)	Lisa Anne Miller	100	Miller's Edge Music	BMI	0:40
				Background Instrumental	
Property Info/Cops Fight (1m19a)	Mark Northam	100	North Edge Music	ASCAP	3:54
				Background Instrumental	
Bit Into The Apple (1m20)	Lisa Anne Miller	100	Miller's Edge Music	BMI	3:57
				Background Instrumental	
Lisa Visits Lyle (1m21)	Mark Northam	100	North Edge Music	ASCAP	3:02
				Background Instrumental	
You Seem Distant (1m22)	Mark Northam	100	North Edge Music	ASCAP	0:57
				Background Instrumental	
Lisa Wants Out (1m23a)	Lisa Anne Miller	100	Miller's Edge Music	BMI	0:39
				Background Instrumental	
End Chase (1m23b)	Lisa Anne Miller	100	Miller's Edge Music	BMI	5:01
				Background Instrumental	
Jake To The Rescue (1m23c)	Mark Northam	100	North Edge Music	ASCAP	3:52
				Background Instrumental	

Sample Performing Rights Cue Sheet (continued)

"MALIBU NIGHTS" Cue Sheet - Page 3 of 3

On The Rocks (1m24)	Lisa Anne Miller	100	Miller's Edge Music	BMI <u>Background Instrumental</u>	3:20
Malibu Nights - E.C. (1m25)	Mark Northam Lisa Anne Miller	50 50	North Edge Music Miller's Edge Music	ASCAP BMI <u>End Title</u>	3:02

TOTAL MUSIC   **1:20:58**

FINAL DELIVERY CUE LIST

Prepared By   Composer, Music Editor, or Engineer

Users   Composer, Music Editor, Film Production Company, Post Production facility

Maintained   In main work file for project. Always send copies to the client with the final delivery tapes and to the music editor. Best to include multiple copies of this document to the post production facility for convenience during prelay and dubbing sessions.

Description   This document is included with your final, mixed music tape. It is designed to show the post production personnel exactly where each piece of music starts, ends, and on which tracks of your tape it is recorded. Any alternate versions and instruments isolated on their own tracks are also noted on this document. Given the frantic pace of today's post production schedule, it is important to make this document clear and easy to understand. You may want to check the format of your document with post production personnel on each project to make sure all information they require is included.

When using a non-time-coded tape format such as DAT, the Final Delivery Cue List becomes even more important since it contains the only time code reference for your music. This document should list all music cues and specify the location on the DAT tape (program ID) and _exactly_ where in the picture (time code location) it should be placed. Information about potential overlaps before or after the cue should be noted on this document for reference by the engineer when transferring the music onto a time-coded format for final mixing.

You may be asked by the post production facility to provide a Dubbing Sheet (shown later in this section). Make sure to ask the post production personnel for the exact form they want this information in, as it can vary widely from one post facility to another. Your music editor should be helpful in preparing whatever delivery documents are needed for a project.

Two important things that will make the post production process easier for everyone (and build allies in the business for you) are:

- Always include a contact name and phone number on your final delivery cue list, track sheets, etc. so it's easy for the post production personnel to get in touch with you if they have any questions (they almost always do!). Always send multiple copies of any documents you send to post production facilities.

- Be as flexible and easy to work with as possible when working with post production facilities and personnel — relationships you build can be very valuable for referrals and future projects.

Sample Final Delivery Cue List #1

WHITE BALLOON
FINAL MUSIC MIX TRACK SHEET

CINEMATRAX
1-888-SCORE-38

Ver 1.0

Cue ID	Title	TC Start	Approx. Length	TRACK CONTENTS - FINAL MUSIC MIX TAPE							
				1	2	3	4	5	6	7	8
1m1	Wedding Band	1:00:07:23	0:20	Claps 1	Claps 2	Hey 1	Hey 2	MIX-L	MIX-R	n/a	n/a
1m2	The Kiss	1:00:23:07	0:13	n/a	n/a	n/a	n/a	n/a	n/a	MIX-L	MIX-R
1m3	Main Title	1:01:12:25	1:03	n/a	n/a	n/a	n/a	MIX-L	MIX-R	n/a	n/a
1m5/6	Check Out the Noise	1:03:44:22	1:52	n/a	n/a	n/a	n/a	MIX-L	MIX-R	Perc Mix-L	Perc Mix-R
1m7	Smoking and Drinking	1:07:04:21	0:21	n/a	n/a	n/a	n/a	Alt Mix1-L	Alt Mix1-R	MIX-L	MIX-R
1m9	Ron Approaches Kim	1:08:59:04	0:52	n/a	n/a	Alt Mix2-L	Alt Mix2-R	Alt Mix1-L	Alt Mix1-R	MIX-L	MIX-R
1m10a	Sticks Story	1:12:03:07	1:02	n/a	n/a	n/a	Dry Stix	Flute Mix-L	Flute Mix-R	Perc Mix-L	Perc Mix-R
1m10b	Rape	1:14:04:17	2:04	n/a	n/a	n/a	Dry Sticks	MIX-L	MIX-R	Wet Sticks-L	Wet Sticks-R
1m11	Why?	1:17:47:16	1:34	MIX-L	MIX-R	Boom Perc-L	Boom Perc-R	Old Ver-L	Old Ver-R	Old Ver Perc-L	Old Ver Perc-R
1m12	Shooting Balloons/E.C.	1:19:41:00	1:20	n/a	n/a	n/a	n/a	Alt Mix-L	Alt Mix-R	MIX-L	MIX-R

NOTES:

1. Tracks marked as "n/a" are blank or contain unused multitrack material and should not be used.
2. Tracks enclosed in rectangles are preferred final mix tracks.
3. Cues with sustained music at end are recorded long to allow for fades during mixing.
4. Cues 1m1 and 1m2 overlap and should be crossfaded.
5. On 1m9 (Ron Approaches Kim), Alt Mix1 is with more flute, and Alt Mix2 is with the flute muted.
6. On 1m11 (Why), "Old Ver" is an old version of the cue, and tracks 1-4 contain the new arrangement of the cue.
7. 1m4 (Jazz Source) is recorded on a separate DAT.
8. Cue 1m8 (Rock Source) was not scored by Cinematrax and is not on this tape.

Sample Final Delivery Cue List #2

CINEMATRAX
1146 N. Central Ave. #103
Glendale, CA 91202
Tel 1-888-SCORE-38

Client: FredWorks Films
Project: "RUNNING HARD"

FINAL MUSIC CUE LIST

SCORE CUES:

#	CUE	TITLE	TC Start	Approx. Timing	DA-88 TRACKS	SAFETY DAT TRACK NO.	Notes
1	1m4	Friends Approach Car	1:05:00:07	0:18	1/2	1	
2	1m8	Dix Sniffs/Bust	1:07:19:23	2:47	1/2	2	
3	1m9	Troy Gets It	1:10:07:03	3:19	3/4	3	
4	1m10	Punching Owner/Escape	1:14:30:28	1:46	1/2	4	
5	1m12	Route 395	1:21:50:18	0:20	1/2	5	
6	1m17	Are We Looking for Dix	1:28:25:08	0:23	1/2	6	
7	1m22	Back at the Station	1:34:13:10	0:33	1/2	7	
8	1m24	Bring Them Back Alive	1:37:42:09	0:38	1/2	8	
9	1m28	Hotel Room	1:43:08:13	2:11	3/4	9	Alt. ver on Tracks 3/4 with no log drums (DAT trk 10)
10	1m31	Dix Waits	1:46:32:00	1:16	1/2	15	
11	1m32/34	Beautiful Canyons/Sunset Love	1:47:48:15	2:29	3/4	25	
12	1m35	Dix Dream/Truck	1:50:17:03	1:21	1/2	11	Alt. ver on DAT trk 12 with no guitar
13	1m38	Marry Me	1:53:38:16	3:18	1/2	24	
14	1m39	Train/Dix/Driving	1:57:14:08	2:17	1/2	23	
15	1m45	Hank Visits Tommy	2:08:11:11	2:21	1/2	17	
16	1m46	Gotta Get Outta Here	2:11:45:07	1:42	5/6	11	
17	1m47	Hank Squeals/Baby/It's Over	2:13:24:13	1:23	3/4	19	
18	1m48	ID Positive	2:14:47:02	0:32	1/2	13	
19	1m49	I Wanted This Kid	2:15:18:26	2:31	3/4	14	
20	1m50	Dix/Fight to Death	2:17:50:08	3:21	1/2	16	
21	1m51	Flying Fall	2:21:11:17	0:32	3/4	20	
22	1m52	He's One of Mine/Revenge	2:21:43:08	0:56	1/2	18	
23	1m53	Tommy's Departure/Water	2:22:47:08	1:04	3/4	21	
24	1m55	Gharrett Lives/End Credits	2:24:51:10	5:09	1/2	26	End of cue is approx. 2:30:00:00

Sample Final Delivery Cue List #3 (non-time code format)

	SHOPPING SPREE Master Music DAT			CINEMATRAX 1-888-SCORE-38

Prog ID	Orig ID	Cue Title	Length	Notes
1	1m6a	Running	2:01	
2	1m6b	Running Button	:01	To be used to end "Running"
3	1m12	Throwing Items	2:00	
4	1m12b	Throwing Items Button	:01	Use at end of "Throwing Items"
5	1m5	The Inspection	:30	
6	1m3	Town Square	:10	
7	1m4	Partner Arrives	:10	
8	1m7	To Commercial	1:30	
9	1m8a/b/c	From Commercial versions A/B/C	:05	
10	1m9	The Winner	:07	
11	1m10a	As the Set Turns	:15	Old version (long)
12	1m13	The Loser - versions A/B/C	:03	Same cue with different mutes
13	1m11b	Prize Theme #2	:45	
14	1m2	The Stores	1:30	
15	1m11a	Prize Theme #1	:45	Replaced by new version at ID 20
16	1m1	Main Title	1:30	
17	1m14	End Credits	3:00	
18	1m10b	As the Set Turns w/sound effects	:15	
19	1m10c	As the Set Turns - new short ver.	:10	
20	none	New Partner inspection	:20	
21	none	Prize Theme #1 - long ver.	1:30	
22	1m5b	Host Inspection	2:00	

DUBBING SHEET

Prepared By   Music Editor (usually) or Engineer

Users   Music Editor, Composer, Post Production Facility

Maintained   Included with all copies of master tapes. Used by post production personnel during music prelay and dubbing sessions.

Description   If you record your final music masters on a time coded multitrack tape format (such as Tascam DA-88 or ADAT), the music editor can create these sheets for each tape. These sheets are used by the post production facility to help determine what music is recorded on which tracks of the tape. It is similar in content to the Final Delivery Cue Sheet, but is in a format commonly used (and asked for) by post production facilities.

Although creating these forms may be additional work that you consider redundant or optional, if the post production facility asks for these sheets, prepare them. Keeping post production personnel happy and on your side can have big benefits during and after your project.

Sample Dubbing Sheet

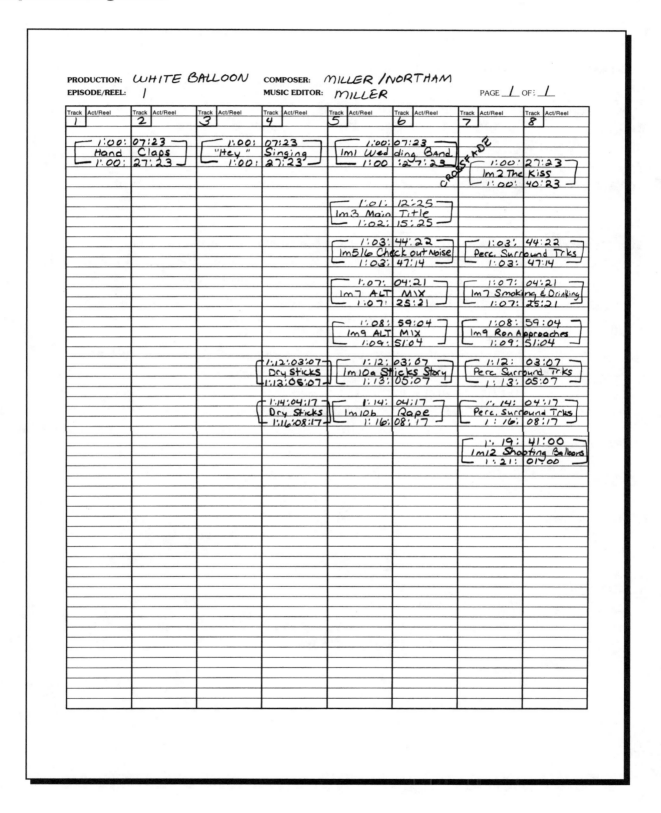

PRODUCTION: WHITE BALLOON **COMPOSER:** MILLER / NORTHAM

EPISODE/REEL: 1 **MUSIC EDITOR:** MILLER PAGE 1 OF 1

Track 1	Act/Reel	Track 2	Act/Reel	Track 3	Act/Reel	Track 4	Act/Reel	Track 5	Act/Reel	Track 6	Act/Reel	Track 7	Act/Reel	Track 8	Act/Reel

1:00:07:23 Hand Claps 1:00:27:23 — 1:00:07:23 "Hey" Singing 1:00:27:23 — 1:00:07:23 1m1 Wedding Band 1:00:27:23 — CROSSFADE 1:00:27:23 1m2 The Kiss 1:00:40:23

1:01:12:25 1m3 Main Title 1:02:15:25

1:03:44:22 1m5/6 Check out Noise 1:03:47:14 — 1:03:44:22 Perc. Surround Trks 1:03:47:14

1:07:04:21 1m7 ALT MIX 1:07:25:21 — 1:07:04:21 1m7 Smoking & Drinking 1:07:25:21

1:08:59:04 1m9 ALT MIX 1:09:51:04 — 1:08:59:04 1m9 Ron Approaches 1:09:51:04

1:12:03:07 Dry Sticks 1:13:05:07 — 1:12:03:07 1m10a Sticks Story 1:13:05:07 — 1:12:03:07 Perc. Surround Trks 1:13:05:07

1:14:04:17 Dry Sticks 1:16:08:17 — 1:14:04:17 1m10b Rape 1:16:08:17 — 1:14:04:17 Perc. Surround Trks 1:16:08:17

1:19:41:00 1m12 Shooting Balloons 1:21:01:00

STUDIO INVENTORY

Prepared By   Composer or Assistant

Users   Composer, Composer's Bank, Insurance Company

Maintained   In permanent asset files, copy maintained off-site in case of disaster

Description   This is a vital document for your studio. It can serve many purposes including documentation for your insurance company, documentation of collateral for your bank, and as a reference when making warranty claims for repairs. We've also found it to be useful when a manufacturer indicates a recall or repair is necessary for equipment within a certain serial number range.

It is important to keep your studio inventory document updated so it lists your current studio setup. Don't forget to include any new equipment you acquire and delete any equipment you sell. Usually equipment loaned to others should remain on the list for insurance purposes, and you may want to include equipment <u>you</u> borrow from others on a long-term basis (with appropriate notes).

Sample Studio Inventory

STUDIO INVENTORY				**CinemaTrax**	
				1146 N. Central Ave. #103	
				Glendale, CA 91202	
				1-888-SCORE-38	

MFG	TYPE	DESCRIPTION	SERIAL NO.	PURCHASE PRICE	INSURED VALUE
AKG	Headphones	Model 240 Headphones (qty 3)	*****	300	300
AKG	Microphone	D3900 Microphone	*****	400	400
Alesis	Effects	3630 Compressor/Limiter	*****	300	300
Apple	Computer	14" Color Monitor	*****	350	350
Apple	Computer	17" Multiscan Color Monitor	*****	1,200	1,200
Apple	Computer	CD300E External CD ROM Drive	*****	400	400
Apple	Computer	Extended Keyboard	*****	100	100
Apple	Computer	Macintosh Classic Computer w/2meg RAM	*****	1,500	1,500
Apple	Computer	Quadra 650 Computer 16meg RAM/230 HD	*****	3,500	3,500
Apple	Computer	Quadra 650 Computer 40megRAM/230 HD	*****	4,000	4,000
Apple	Printer	Select 360 Laser Printer	*****	1,500	1,500
Apple	Speakers	Stereo Computer Speakers	*****	150	150
APS	Disk Drive	850 Meg Hard Drive for Roland Sampler	*****	600	600
Ashley	Amplifier	CFT-1800 Power Amplifier	*****	700	700
Atari	Computer	SC1224 RGB Color Monitor	*****	250	250
Audix	Speakers	Model 1A Speakers (qty 2)	*****	500	500
Brunswick Instr.	Accessory	Click Kicker click generator	*****	450	450
Countryman	Accessory	Type 85 FET Direct Box	*****	250	250
DBX	Effects	Project 1 Stereo Reverb Unit	*****	350	350
Digidesign	Computer	Audiomedia II Digital Sound Card	*****	1,100	1,100
DOD	Effects	Graphic Equalizer Model 831 series II	*****	175	175
E-Mu	Sound Module	Proformance/1 w/Upgrade Chip	*****	500	500
E-Mu	Sound Module	Proteus/2	*****	800	800
E-Mu	Sound Module	Proteus/2	*****	800	800
Furman	Accessory	PL-PLUS Power Conditioners (qty 4)	*****	500	500
Furman	PB-40	Patch Bay (1/4" -> 1/4")	*****	140	140
Furman	PB-40	Patch Bay (1/4" -> 1/4")	*****	140	140
Furman	PB-40	Patch Bay (1/4" -> 1/4")	*****	140	140
Furman	PB-40	Patch Bay (1/4" -> 1/4")	*****	140	140
Gentner	Accessory	SPB-3A Telephone Interface	*****	650	650
Glyph	Disk Drive	Rackmount Jaz Drive Model GJZ-1000R	*****	700	700
Glyph	Disk Drive	Desktop Jaz Drive Model GJZ-1000S	*****	600	600
Hamilton	Accessory	Metal Music Stand (qty 4)	*****	140	140
Hewlett Packard	Computer	HP Deskwriter printer	*****	250	250
Horita	Accessory	Blackburst Generator Model BSG-50	*****	250	250
Iomega	Disk Storage	1 Gigabyte Jaz Carts (qty 6)	*****	800	800
JL Cooper	Accessory	Media Control Station	*****	200	200
Kawai	Amplifier	Keyboard Amp Model KM-20	*****	150	150
Kawai	Keyboard	Synthesizer Model K1	*****	450	450
Kensington	Computer	MasterPiece Plus power distribution mod	*****	150	150
Kensington	Computer	TurboMouse	*****	125	125
Kenwood	Tape Recorder	Cassette Recorder	*****	230	230
KK Systems	Equipment Rack	Dual Column 40-space Rack Enclosure	*****	900	900
KMD	Accessory	Tripod Boom mic stands - black (qty 12)	*****	700	700
KMD	Accessory	Tripod mic stand - black (qty 4)	*****	160	160
Korg	Sound Module	01R/W Synthesizer Module	*****	1,500	1,500

SECTION III
FINANCES, CONTRACTS AND AGREEMENTS

This section contains information on the finances and legal aspects of your film and television music business. We've presented the documents and examples in the order that you might expect to use them as part of a project. We're very fortunate to have the assistance and advice of Mr. Steve Winogradsky, one of the leading attorneys in the world of film and television music, who has reviewed the agreements and licenses presented in this section.

The documents and agreements presented in this section are:

Music Production Budget — used as a tool to calculate fees for a project, especially when working with a *package* deal or when in fee negotiations with a client or potential client. Usually this document is very detailed and contains information about all costs for a music production.

Music Production Proposal — a summary or outline of all the services and products included in a proposed music production budget. Used more as a presentation, this document can help a potential client make his/her decision about the music needs of a project.

Letter of Agreement — a letter used when initially making a commitment to score a film or television project. It documents agreement on certain points of a deal or negotiation and expresses an intent to further discuss the remaining deal points.

Deal Memo — an outline of a negotiated deal which is agreed to by both parties and includes all of the major deal points such as screen credit, publishing assignment, payment schedule, and delivery dates.

Composer Agreement — a detailed contract for the services of a composer. Contracts can vary greatly depending on the negotiating power of the composer and his/her agent, and on whether or not the deal is a *package* deal.

Synchronization License — used when a publisher allows use of their music in a film or television project. With this license the filmmaker can record the publisher's music *in sync* with his/her picture. This is an important document for composers to be aware of when they retain the publishing on their compositions because it needs to be issued in conjunction with the Composer Agreement.

Master Use License — allows a filmmaker to use a specific sound recording in conjunction with his/her film, television project or soundtrack. The owner of the sound recording (usually a record company, publisher, or individual composer) would issue the Master Use License to the filmmaker.

Sync Use Quote Request Letter / Master Use Quote Request Letter — these are documents that can be used when requesting quotes for Synchronization or Master Use Licenses from other publishers or record companies. These letters are useful if you need to get rate information for licensing music and/or recordings.

Independent Contractor Agreement for Musicians — this form can be used to document the intent of a musician to be treated as an independent contractor for tax purposes, and to receive no future payments or royalties for his/her services.

There are two types of deal structures that are commonly used when negotiating with a composer to create a score for a film or television project. These are the **Package Deal** and the **Composing Fee Deal** structures, which are described below and are referenced later in the section on Composer Agreements.

Package Deal (also known as an *All-In* deal) — In a Package Deal, the composer is responsible for all costs involved in composing, arranging, orchestrating, recording, and delivering the final music master tapes. Under this type of arrangement, the composer must be very careful when negotiating costs he/she will incur such as recording studio time, musicians, orchestration, and copying, since those costs will come directly out of his/her fees for the project. The composer bears 100% of the responsibility for these costs, and must continually work to make sure that costs do not become excessive. Package Deals are very common in low and medium budget films, and are becoming very common in television work. Now that most composers own MIDI sampler/synthesizer-based studios, this kind of agreement will probably continue to grow in popularity as the costs of projects move more and more into the composer's domain. In a Package Deal, you should try to exclude costs that are beyond your control, such as on-camera/sideline musician services, vocalists requested by the producer, and licensing of previously copyrighted compositions.

Composing Fee Deal — A Composing Fee Deal is an agreement for composing services only. This type of deal sometimes includes the services of orchestrators in the composer's fee package, but this is a negotiable point. Under this type of deal the film production company bears the responsibility for all costs involved in the arranging, orchestrating and recording of the music. Typically, the film production company will have existing relationships with music contractors (to hire the musicians), music preparation companies (to prepare the score and parts for the musicians), and recording studios. The composer may or may not have input as to who is hired for these jobs.

As part of the section on Composer Agreements, we have also included an **Analysis of Contract Sections** to help further explain the Composer Agreement. We describe the major sections of a typical Composer Agreement, and describe why certain language is used and when you should consider using it.

Another important document to be aware of is **The Musicians Union Assumption Agreement**. Whenever union musicians are used for a film or television project in the United States, the Musicians Union (The American Federation of Musicians) requires that an Assumption Agreement be completed. The Assumption Agreement is a contract between the union and the *signatory* company, and requires the signatory company signing the agreement to be responsible for possible future payments to the musicians. These payments can be triggered by the commercial success of a picture or distribution of the production in different forms. The union will not permit recording sessions to occur unless the document is signed. The composer should <u>always</u> insist that the film or television production company be the signatory on any Assumption Agreement that is created for a project.

<u>It is extremely inadvisable for any composer to sign as the signatory on an Assumption Agreement because the composer is in no position to control the future distribution and usage of the film and its music, yet would be responsible for all future payments to the musicians.</u>

When using a payroll service for union recordings, the payroll service may technically act as the employer but will require an Assumption Agreement. The same hazard exists in this situation — whoever signs the Assumption Agreement as signatory is liable for all future payments to the musicians. Even if the composer has some sort of reciprocal agreement with the film company that reimburses the composer for all future payments and expenses, the risk exists that the film company may no longer be in business or may not honor the agreement. In all cases, the Musicians Union holds the signatory responsible for all future special and new-use payments to the musicians.

MUSIC PRODUCTION BUDGET

Prepared By   Composer, Agent or Manager, or Contractor

When to Use   When you have interest in a specific project from a potential client and are ready, or will be ready to talk about finances with a potential client

Description   The music budget for a project is almost always the first financial document created once you are being seriously considered for a project. In some cases you will be given a total budget figure by your potential client. In other cases you'll be asked for a *quote* or budget. In either case, the music budget is the best way to prepare yourself for the negotiating phase of a project. Only by preparing an accurate, realistic, and complete budget will you really be able to negotiate from a position of knowledge.

During negotiations you may be asked how much money should be allotted for live musicians and associated expenses such as the recording studio, engineer, and tape costs. You also may be faced with the question of whether or not to record under a union (Musicians Union) contract. Depending on whether or not you are working under a Package Deal, these questions may have a significant impact on your fees and profit on the project. Once you start putting your music budget together you'll be able to answer these questions quickly.

Sometimes you may be in the position of needing to substantiate the package fees you are asking from the client. Specifically, you may need to show that a significant portion of the package fees are going towards musician expenses (as opposed to your own creative fees). Your music budget is evidence of these intentions which can be documented to your client if desired.

Finally, it is important to separate *fixed* costs such as your creative fees from *variable* costs like the music editor fees (if you are paying these), musicians, engineers, and the recording studio. This is the best way to prevent budget negotiations from reducing your creative fees in a Package Deal scenario. Also, don't forget to include all relevant expenses, no matter how small. Good examples of expenses that are often not included in music budgets but should be are food and drinks during recording sessions, tape costs, messenger and delivery expenses, and materials needed for demos as the project progresses such as video and audio tapes.

When hiring union musicians, it is almost always to your advantage to hire a music contractor. A music contractor hires musicians based on your input and requirements, and handles all necessary paperwork that will be required by the Musicians Union and the payroll service being used. A music contractor can be especially helpful in putting together an orchestra or group of musicians that work well together. Also, most major contractors have good relationships with the legal and contract departments of the Musicians Union. For smaller groups, the leader of the musical group often will function as the contractor. For larger groups (ten or more musicians) you will probably want to hire a professional music contractor. The Musicians Union can provide a list of contractors in your area.

We've included some different versions of music production budgets for a variety of projects. We usually start a new music budget by using one from another project that is similar in size and scope. We then customize the budget as necessary depending on the number of musicians, time estimates, and extra costs for that project.

For many higher budget feature films, the total music budget including music supervision, songs, score, and recording costs is often 8 - 10% of the film budget.

Sample Music Production Budget #1 (Union, Television Main Title)

CinemaTrax
Production Budget - Television

Project: **Main Title for a cable series**

Date: 12/15/94
Version: 3

Talent:	Union	Scale Wages	Pension	Health & Welfare	TOTAL WAGES	TOTALS
Piano/Leader	AF of M	$357.30	$32.16	$9.00	$398.46	
Bass	AF of M	$178.65	$16.08	$9.00	$203.73	
Brass Player 1	AF of M	$178.65	$16.08	$9.00	$203.73	
Brass Player 2	AF of M	$178.65	$16.08	$9.00	$203.73	
Guitar	AF of M	$178.65	$16.08	$9.00	$203.73	
Music Prep/Copying	AF of M	$132.14	$11.89	$9.00	$153.03	
TOTAL AF of M	AF of M	$1,204.04	$108.37	$54.00	$1,366.41	**$1,366.41**
TAXES (15%)	AF of M					$180.61
AF of M Payroll Co.	AF of M				2.5% handling fee	$30.10
*Vocalist (2 tracks)	SAG	$2,702.00	$345.86		taxes based on Texas rates	$3,047.86
TAXES (17.59%)	SAG					$475.28
SAG Payroll Co.	SAG				$7.50 per check handling fee	$7.50
Recording Studio					6 hours @ $75.00	$450.00
Tape Costs					(1) 24 track tape & (1) DAT	$151.54
Equipment rental					(1) DA-88 digital 8 track	$75.00
Production Fee						$5,000.00
Contingency fee (10%)						$1,078.43

TOTAL ESTIMATED COST $11,862.72

*Vocalist rate is $1,351.00 per track

NOTES:
1) Production company to function as AF of M and SAG signatory and will sign appropriate assumption agreements.
2) Production company to receive all tape masters including 24 track master.
3) Timings on Final version to be the same as Demo versions previously submitted.
4) Production company to provide any applicable time code information to be striped on 24 track or final DAT master.

Sample Music Production Budget #2 (Non-Union, Low Budget Feature Film)

Project:	Low-Budget Feature Film (Video Release)
Date:	August 15, 1996
Description:	approx. 60 minutes of music

Musicians

Qty	Description	No. of Sessions	Cost per Session	Cartage or Extra Pay	Total Cost
1	Violin/Contractor	4	300	0	1,200.00
2	Violins	4	150	0	1,200.00
1	Cello	4	150	0	600.00
1	Trumpet	2	150	0	300.00
1	French Horn	1	150	0	150.00
1	Trombone	2	150	0	300.00
1	Woodwind	3	150	0	450.00
1	Percussionist	1	150	100	250.00
	TOTAL MUSICIAN COSTS				**$4,450.00**

Creative Costs

Description	Total Cost
Composing, Orchestrating and Production of music	5000
TOTAL CREATIVE COSTS	**$5,000.00**

Production Costs

Description	No. of Hours	Cost/Hour	Cost/Each	Total Cost
Music Editor (limited duties)				750.00
Music Preparation				900.00
Recording Engineer				1,350.00
Recording Studio - outside studio (1 day)				800.00
Tape Costs				125.00
Equipment Rental				200.00
Miscellaneous Costs (food, messenger costs, etc.)				50.00
TOTAL PRODUCTION COSTS				**$4,175.00**

SUBTOTAL		$13,625.00
Contingency	10%	$1,362.50
TOTAL PROJECT BUDGET		$14,987.50

Notes

1. Will begin starting 8/22/96
2. Demos delivered with video at the end of each week
3. Recording sessions 9/20-9/21
4. Final delivery of all music masters on 9/24/96

Sample Music Production Budget #3 (Non-Union, National Radio Package)

CinemaTrax		
Production Budget - Non-Union		**Date: 6/12/95**
		Version: FINAL
PROJECT: National Radio Music Campaign :30, :30, :60		

Talent:		FINAL AMOUNT
Concertmaster		$250
Violin 2		$150
Violin 3		$150
Violin 4		$150
Violin 5		$150
Violin 6		$150
Cello 1		$150
Cello 2		$150
Bass (incl. cartage)		$150
Woodwind 1		$150
Woodwind 2		$150
Trumpet 1		$150
Trumpet 2		$150
Trombone		$150
Percussionist (incl. cartage)		$250
Harp (incl. cartage)		$200
Contractor		$200
TOTAL MUSICIAN/CONTRACTOR COSTS		**$2,850**
PRODUCTION:		
Copyist		$325
Recording Studio	7 hours @ $75	$525
Engineer	8 hours @ $40	$320
Tape Costs		$23
DA-88 Rental		$75
Assistant		$50
TOTAL PRODUCTION COSTS		**$1,318**
TOTAL PROJECT COSTS:		**$4,168**

SUMMARY	
Total Revenue	$7,500.00
Less Costs	($4,168.00)
Total Profit	**$3,332.00**

MUSIC PRODUCTION PROPOSAL

Prepared By   Composer, Agent or Manager

When to Use   When a potential client has expressed interest in your services and wants to know what will be included in your fees

Description   A Music Production Proposal can be used for smaller scale projects such as a single song or theme and can be used when you want to give the client an overview of the budget (rather than all the details). We use a Package Proposal when dealing with executives and people who may not want to see all the fine print of the budget such as which musician gets paid what. A Music Production Proposal also works well when you are asked for a *proposal* and the client is trying to decide whether to do the project or whether to use you for the project.

Use a Music Budget when you want to provide lots of detail to justify the music fees you're negotiating. Use a Music Production Proposal when you want to do more of a presentation which emphasizes your overall selling points and advantages.

Sample Music Production Proposal

Music Production Proposal
Cable Network Promotional CD (1 cut)

This music production proposal includes all costs associated with producing completed instrumental music tracks for the project, including arranging, orchestrating, recording and preparation of DA-88 tapes for use in live recording sessions. Proposal price also includes live musician orchestrations as indicated below.

Total arranger/orchestration fees: $2,500 (not including live musicians costs)

Includes:
- all synth tracks fully arranged, orchestrated, and recorded
- complete synth demos of final arrangement before final production
- fully produced tracks featuring state-of-the-art electronic samples
- recording (synth tracks) to 16 tracks of DA-88 tape
- orchestrations for live violins, woodwinds, and horns
- conducting for live musician recording sessions
- lead sheet prepared

Additional:
- Credit to be provided for arrangements used on album
- Rehearsal services (onsite) at $75/hr plus travel, billed separately
- Music preparation (parts for live musicians) will be billed at actual cost from copyist, and will be based on number of live musicians used
- Cinematrax studio facilities available for live musician recording and final mixing at $75/hr
- Engineer required for live recording and mixing at $50/hr, billed separately
- Musician fees, billed separately - estimatated (non-union):

4 Violins - 2 hours of recording	*480.00*
1 Woodwind doubler - 2 hours	*120.00*
2 horn players - 2 hours	*240.00*

Payment terms: Initial payment of $1,250.00 due upon start of work
Balance of $1,250.00 due upon delivery of music tracks

1146 N. Central Ave. #103 ✦ GLENDALE, CA 91202
TELEPHONE: 1-888-SCORE-38 ✦ INTERNET: www.cinematrax.com

LETTER OF AGREEMENT

Prepared By Composer, Agent, Manager, or Attorney

When To Use When you want to document that agreement has been reached on some major points of a deal. It is an optional letter that can be used when you are first making a commitment to score a film or television project.

Description Agreement Letters specify the points of a deal and issues that were discussed and agreed to, but usually does not completely define or outline the entire deal or agreement. The Agreement Letter is useful for confirming a discussion you've had with a filmmaker in writing. It is not a substitute for a Deal Memo or Composer Agreement/Contract, since an Agreement Letter usually doesn't describe the deal in full. Once all the major points have been agreed upon, use a Deal Memo to document that the deal has been *closed*.

Sample Letter of Agreement

Calvin Composer
2359 Santa Monica Boulevard #911
Los Angeles, CA 90099
(310) 555-2368

Mr. Fred Filmmaker
Fred Films Works, Inc.
9999 Sunset Boulevard
Suite 007
Los Angeles, CA   90099

Dear Mr. Filmmaker:

This will confirm our agreement to provide a musical score for your film *Fred's Nightmare* at a package price of $50,000. We will be responsible for writing and recording all score for the film per our discussions.

Although this fee does not include source music or songs, we will be happy to assist you in locating and retaining a qualified Music Supervisor for these tasks.

I'll send over a deal memo which goes into specific details for your score, but in the meantime please don't hesitate to call me if you have any questions or if I can provide any further information.

Sincerely,

Calvin Composer

DEAL MEMO

Prepared By   Composer, Agent, Manager, or Attorney

When to Use   When all the major points of a deal have been agreed to. It is a good policy to document agreements as soon as they occur. In the case of a Deal Memo, this becomes even more important as the Composer Agreement or Contract may not be prepared until after work and payments have begun for a project.

Description   Deal Memos serve to document the agreement reached between a composer and a production company. The Deal Memo will usually be the basis for the Composer Agreement, so it should document all key negotiating points such as screen credit, publishing (ownership) assignment, payment schedule, and delivery dates for your work tapes and final music master tapes. Both the client and the composer should sign the Deal Memo. Until the final contract or agreement is prepared, the Deal Memo can have the effect of a binding contract (consult your attorney for specifics on contracts).

Because of the complexities of today's legal climate, you may often be asked to begin work on a project based on a Deal Memo and initial payment. This is often the case when you are dealing with a film production company that prepares its own Composer Agreements. Since you don't want to do anything to delay or disrupt the project, you may not want to balk at starting work without a Composer Agreement. The Deal Memo can be used to document the points of your deal for later reference and to get the client's signed approval without having to wait for their legal department to complete the Composer Agreement.

In some cases if you are working with an agent, your agent may sign a Deal Memo on your behalf. If you have given your agent appropriate power of attorney (see your attorney for more details on this), your agent may be able to commit you to a deal by signing a Deal Memo. Make sure you have a clear understanding with your agent or manager about when and how he/she can or cannot commit you to deals. If you are represented by an agent, it is customary for the agent to prepare the Deal Memo, and for the agent to receive all monies on your behalf.

The most important aspect of a Deal Memo is that it should contain <u>all the key points of agreement that have been made between the composer and filmmaker</u>. Any negotiating points or deal considerations that are not included in the Deal Memo may be very difficult to negotiate after the music has been completed and delivered.

Sample Deal Memo

Calvin Composer
2359 Santa Monica Boulevard #911
Los Angeles, CA 90099
(310) 555-2368

January 1, 1997

Mr. Fred Filmmaker
Fred Film Works, Inc.
9999 Sunset Boulevard
Suite 007
Los Angeles, CA 90099

RE: for services of Calvin Composer / *Fred's Nightmare* Feature Film

Dear Mr. Filmmaker:

The following will set forth the basic terms of our agreement to furnish
to Fred Film Works, Inc. (Producer) the services of Calvin Composer
(Composer) to package the musical score for the film referenced above:

1.   SERVICES: To package the score for *Fred's Nightmare* including
all   costs incurred in the recording and delivery of the master, excluding   the following costs:

  A)   Music Editors (other than those employed by composer)
  B)   Mag stock and transfers, including transfers of any kind
  C)   Licensing of music not composed by Calvin Composer
  D)   Re-scoring i.e. re-recording required for creative rea-
  sons   outside control of Composer after delivery
  of the master.
  E)   Lyricist and vocalist related expenses
  F)   Pre-score (other than that agreed upon by composer)

2.   PACKAGE FEE: $50,000

3.   PAYMENT SCHEDULE: $25,000 upon commencement of services
                 $12,500 upon commencement of recording
                 $12,500 upon delivery of music master record-
ings

Mr. Fred Filmmaker
January 1, 1997
Page Two

4.　　<u>SCREEN CREDIT</u>:　In the main titles on a separate card to read:

MUSIC BY
CALVIN COMPOSER

5.　　<u>PAID ADVERTISING</u>:　Credit as set forth above to appear in paid
advertisements at Producer's discretion

6.　　<u>PUBLISHING</u>:　Composer shall retain ownership of publishing
rights and　　royalties on all music composed by Composer under this
agreement.　　　Composer to provide client with appropriate sync
licenses to permit　　　use of music as described herein.

All monies and correspondence should be directed to:

Calvin Composer
2359 Santa Monica Boulevard #911
Los Angeles, CA 90099
(310) 555-2368

Calvin Composer is affiliated with ASCAP
Social Security No:　007-12-3456

Best Regards,

Calvin Composer

Agreed and Accepted By Fred Film Works, Inc. by:

_____

Fred Filmmaker

COMPOSER AGREEMENT

Prepared By   Composer, Film Production Company, Composer's Lawyer, Agent or Manager

When to Use   A Composer Agreement is used to document all the terms of a deal in detail. It is usually required by the legal department of the film or television production company, and may be required to be completed before work or payments begin.

Description   Once you have agreed to work on a project, a Deal Memo is usually signed. At that point an initial payment is made and the Deal Memo usually states that a complete agreement or contract will be created that describes all the deal points and agreement issues in detail.

You will either be asked to send the client an agreement (you must prepare the Composer Agreement) or you will be sent a contract by the client. For our examples, we use the words *contract* and *agreement* interchangeably. For lower budget projects, you may often be asked to supply the client with a Composer Agreement that you create. We've included some major points that should be included in *every* Composer Agreement and a detailed explanation of the sections of a typical Composer Agreement.

If you are given a Composer Agreement or Contract created by a filmmaker's production company, make sure to have your attorney examine it carefully. These types of contracts <u>always</u> favor your client, so you should carefully examine what you are being asked to do, how much and when you will be paid, and who will retain important future revenue such as performing rights writers and publishers royalties, mechanical payments on CDs and videotape sales, and any monies the filmmaker might receive by licensing the music to others.

One of the most important issues you will face when starting in the business and doing low budget projects is the question of who will retain the publishing rights (effectively, the ownership of the music) and the master rights (the ownership of the sound recordings) of the music you write. Many composers attempt to retain the publishing and master rights when composing fees are low so they can re-license the music to others and attempt to derive other income from the music. A very popular way to do this is to release a soundtrack album for the film or television project and take advantage of the many film and television music collectors that purchase this kind of product. Also, since the publisher's performing rights royalties are equal to the writer's, owning the publishing effectively doubles your performing rights royalty income from that music.

We've included a step-by-step description of a typical Composer Agreement, including versions where the composer retains publishing and the client retains publishing. Since every Composer Agreement is unique, you should consider the ideas presented here as a basis or starting point only. In any case, you should have your attorney look over any Composer Agreement you create or receive before signing it.

Composer Agreements often have to be constructed from standard paragraphs or language that you maintain on file. We've presented the Composer Agreements as sections, and along with each section have included a description of why the language is used and when you should consider using it. We've also included optional clauses for different situations (package vs. non-package, composer retains publishing vs. client retains publishing), so take some time and carefully decide which sections you want to use based on what you've negotiated with your client. If you're examining a client-supplied Composer Agreement, you may want to compare their text to the sample text presented here to help you understand the agreement better.

The Major Sections of a typical Composer Agreement include:

Header and Introduction	Defines who the agreement is between and the name of the film.
Description of Services	Defines what services are to be rendered and who will pay for recording costs, copyists, orchestrators, and other costs
First Priority to Film during Agreement	Obligates the composer to give first priority to this project during the term of the agreement.
Disposition of Score	States that the producer has no obligation to accept, use, or promote the score in any way. This allows the producer to reject any or all parts of the score, however the composer is almost always paid for work completed in this event.
Compensation	Specifies compensation to the composer and a payment schedule.
Screen Credit	Describes what screen credit(s) will be given to composer.

Music Publishing

Defines who will own the publishing rights to the music.

Performing Rights Royalties

Specifies to whom the writer and publishing performing rights royalties will be paid.

Master Rights Ownership

Specifies who will own the sound recordings of the music.

Rights/Work For Hire/Copyright

Defines the author of the score for copyright purposes.

Other Royalties and Payments

Specifies additional royalties to be paid to the composer by the filmmaker, as the owner of the music, if the music is further exploited in various ways (such as sales of sheet music, synchronized to other film or television projects, soundtrack albums)

Synchronization/Master Licenses

Specifies that the composer will grant the filmmaker appropriate Synchronization and Master Use Licenses in order to use the music in the film. This is necessary only if the composer will retain ownership of the publishing and master rights for the music.

Soundtrack Album Royalties

Includes information on how much the composer will be paid in royalties from soundtrack album sales.

Paid Advertising/Name and Likeness

Documents how and when the filmmaker will include the composer's name and likeness (such as pictures or biographies) in advertising for the film.

Warranty/Certificate of Authorship

The composer states that the music is original and does not infringe upon the rights or copyrights of others. The composer takes legal responsibility for originality of the music.

FINANCES, CONTRACTS AND AGREEMENTS

SAMPLE COMPOSER AGREEMENTS

We've included two typical Composer Agreements for analysis. Listed with each sample agreement are the terms and conditions the agreement was created to address. Following the sample agreements is a detailed analysis of each section of a typical Composer Agreement.

Sample Composer Agreement #1
Package Deal, Composer Retains Publishing

Following is a sample of a *Package Deal* Composer Agreement. In this particular example, the following conditions exist:

1. The composer will retain publishing of the music.

2. The film is a package deal (composer pays all costs of composing, arranging, recording, and delivering the music).

3. The dates for delivery of the time code work tape, demos, and final music tapes are known.

4. The agreement is between Calvin Composer (as a sole proprietor or individual, not a corporation or partnership) and the filmmaker's production company, Fred Film Works, Inc.

5. The package price is $50,000.

6. The sole composer (Calvin Composer) will receive 100% of the performing rights writer and publisher royalties. The composer's publishing company (CalvinWorks Publishing Co.) will own 100% of the music, and will grant to Fred Film Works, Inc. Synchronization and Master Use Rights for use of the music in the film.

Calvin Composer
2359 Santa Monica Boulevard #911
Los Angeles, CA 90099
(310) 555-2368

January 1, 1997

Mr. Fred Filmmaker
Fred Film Works, Inc.
9999 Sunset Boulevard
Suite 007
Los Angeles, CA 90099

Dear Mr. Filmmaker:

Thanks for the opportunity to work with you on *Fred's Nightmare*. The following will outline the agreement between Fred Film Works, Inc. ("Producer") and Calvin Composer ("Composer") in conjunction with the motion picture currently entitled *Fred's Nightmare* ("Film").

Services: Producer hereby engages Composer as an independent contractor to write, compose, arrange, adapt, score, orchestrate, produce, conduct, record, complete and deliver the instrumental score to be used in conjunction with the motion picture *Fred's Nightmare* (hereinafter called "Score") including all costs incurred in the creation, production and delivery of the music master recordings. The score will include all underscore and non-vocal source music under the direction and approval of Producer. The following costs are excluded from the score package and are not subject to this agreement:

(a)   Mag stock
(b)   Licensing of music not composed by Calvin Composer
(c)   Music Editor services (other than those contracted by composer)
(d)   Vocalists requested by producer
(e)   On-camera and/or "sidelining" musicians
(f)   Re-use, New Use, and all Residual payments to musicians

Composer agrees to orchestrate, score, and conduct at all music recording sessions, supervise all scoring and music mixing sessions, arrange for studio time and copying, and arrange for such other services and elements as may be required in connection with the Score.

First Priority to Film: Composer agrees to give this project "first priority" during the term of this agreement and not expend substantial efforts on other composing work.

Disposition of Score: Producer reserves the right not to accept, use, or promote in any way the Score as provided by Composer. Producer reserves the right to request and Composer agrees to make such changes as Producer deems appropriate in the Score prior to delivery.

Delivery: Composer will deliver final music mix recordings as follows:

(a)   Producer will provide Composer with time code work tape containing the final edit ("locked" picture) no later than January 10, 1997.

(b)   Composer will prepare synthesizer demos of principal cues and themes for review by Producer no later than January 24, 1997. Producer agrees to provide any notes or corrections based on these demos to Composer no later than January 27, 1997.

(c)   Composer agrees to deliver final music mix recordings no later than February 10, 1997.

(d)   Producer to specify tape format and any other technical details for final music mix delivery.

Compensation: Producer agrees to a fee of $50,000, payable as follows:

$25,000   payable upon execution of this agreement or commencement of work, whichever comes first;

$12,500   payable upon commencement of recording sessions and

$12,500   payable upon delivery of music master recordings

All payments should be sent to Calvin Composer at the address included at the end of this agreement.

Screen Credit: Single Card Credit in the Main title of the picture on a separate card to read:

Music Composed and Conducted By
Calvin Composer

Size and placement at the Producer's discretion, however size to be no less favorable than that afforded the Director or Writer.

Music Publishing and Performing Rights Royalties: The music publishing company designated for the Score will be CalvinWorks Publishing (ASCAP). CalvinWorks Publishing will own 100% of all worldwide music publishing rights for the Score as described herein. Producer agrees to specify Calvin Composer (ASCAP) as 100% writer and CalvinWorks Publishing (ASCAP) as 100% publisher for all music composed by Calvin Composer on performing rights cue sheets. Producer agrees to prepare accurate performing rights cue sheets and file with ASCAP and provide a copy to Composer and CalvinWorks Publishing no later than 30 days after the sound mix of the film. Producer agrees that all music provided by Composer that is rejected or not used in the final version of *Fred's*

Nightmare shall remain the property of and 100% owned by composer.

Ownership of Sound Recordings: The owner of the final sound recordings for all music used in the Film will be CalvinWorks Publishing (ASCAP). CalvinWorks Publishing will own 100% of all worldwide master rights to all music written by Calvin Composer used in the Film.

Originality and Copyright Considerations: Composer certifies that Composer wrote, composed, arranged, adapted, scored, orchestrated, produced, recorded, completed and delivered the musical works described herein (the Score) as an independent contractor engaged by Producer. Composer certifies that the Score is wholly original with Composer, except to the extent that it is based on or uses material in the public domain or material furnished to Composer by Producer, and that Composer is the author at law thereof and owns all right, title, and interest in and to the Score and the results of Composer's services rendered in connection therewith, including without limitation all copyrights and renewals and extensions of copyrights therein.

Synchronization and Master Licenses for Score: Composer shall grant Producer and its successors, assigns, and licenses the irrevocable right, privilege and authority to record, copy, sell, distribute, and perform the score subject to the terms of the Synchronization and Master Licenses supplied with this document.

Paid Advertising: Producer will make best efforts for composer credit, as set forth above, to appear in all advertisements for the film, including print, broadcast, and other forms of advertising. Size and placement at Producer's discretion, however in no case shall size and placement be less favorable than that afforded to the writer of the film.

Name and Likeness: Composer hereby grants to Producer the non-exclusive right in perpetuity to use and grant to others the right to use Composer's name and likeness in any and all media in connection with Composer's services under this Agreement.

Warranty and Certificate of Authorship: Composer represents and warrants to Producer that (i) Composer has full right and legal capacity to execute and fully perform this Agreement and to make the grants, assignments and waivers contained in it, (ii) that Composer warrants and confirms they he is the sole writer of the original musical compositions ("Score") delivered to Producer for use in the film and that the Score will not be copied from or based on, in whole or in part, any other work; (iii) to the best of Composer's knowledge as far as Composer knows or should have known in the exercise of due diligence and prudence, nothing in the Score does or will infringe on any property right (copyright, trademark, patent right, right to ideas and the like) or personal right (defamation, false light, moral right and the like) of any person or legal entity; and (iv) there is no pending or threatened claim, litigation, arbitration, action or proceeding with respect to the Score. Composer will indemnify and hold harmless Producer, its affiliated companies, successors and assigns, and their respective directors, employees and agents, from and against any claim, loss, liability, damages or judgements, including reasonable outside attorneys' fees, arising from any breach of the above representations and warranties.

This agreement will inure to the benefit of Producer's successors, assigns, lessees, and licensees. Composer will execute, acknowledge and deliver such additional instruments as necessary to confirm the intent of this Agreement.

This instrument is the entire Agreement between the parties and cannot be modified except by a written instrument signed by the Composer and an authorized officer of the Producer.

This Agreement shall be governed by and construed under and in accordance with the laws of the State of California applicable to agreements wholly performed therein.

Agreed to and accepted by the following parties on this _____ day of _____, 1997.

PRODUCER   **COMPOSER**

_____   _____
Fred Filmmaker   Calvin Composer
Fred Film Works, Inc.   2359 Santa Monica Boulevard #911
9999 Sunset Boulevard   Los Angeles, CA 90099
Suite 007
Los Angeles, CA 90099

Sample Composer Agreement #2
Non-Package Deal, Producer Retains Publishing

Following is a sample of a *Composer Fee Only* Composer Agreement. In this particular example, the following conditions exist:

1. The filmmaker will retain publishing of the music.

2. The film is a *composer fee only* deal — all additional costs, including orchestration, recording studio, musicians, and other similar costs are paid for by the filmmaker.

3. The dates for delivery of the time code work tape, demos, and final music tapes are known.

4. The agreement is between Calvin Composer (as a sole proprietor or individual, not a corporation or partnership) and the filmmaker's production company, Fred Film Works, Inc.

5. The composer fee is $75,000.

6. The sole composer (Calvin Composer) will receive 100% of the performing rights writer's royalties. The filmmaker's publishing company (FredFilm Music Publishing Co.) will receive 100% of the publisher's performing rights royalties and will own 100% of the music.

Calvin Composer
2359 Santa Monica Boulevard #911
Los Angeles, CA 90099
(310) 555-2368

January 1, 1997

Mr. Fred Filmmaker
Fred Film Works, Inc.
9999 Sunset Boulevard
Suite 007
Los Angeles, CA 90099

Dear Mr. Filmmaker:

Thanks for the opportunity to work with you on *Fred's Nightmare*. The following will outline the agreement between Fred Film Works, Inc. ("Producer") and Calvin Composer ("Composer") in conjunction with the motion picture currently entitled *Fred's Nightmare* ("Film").

   Services: Producer hereby engages Composer as an independent contractor to compose the score for *Fred's Nightmare* (hereinafter called "Score") including all underscore and non-vocal source music under the direction and approval of Producer.

Producer agrees to pay for all production costs incurred in the orchestration and recording of score including but not limited to the following:

   (a)   Orchestrator(s)
   (b)   Music Preparation Services (including copyists)
   (c)   Recording Costs (including musicians, applicable union benefits and payments, and all studio and recording session costs)
   (d)   Media Costs (including all tape costs and storage costs)
   (e)   Vocalists requested by producer
   (f)   On-camera and/or "sidelining" musicians
   (g)   Re-use, New Use, and all Residual payments to musicians

Producer reserves the exclusive right to choose, negotiate, and approve any and all costs incurred in the orchestration and recording of the score.

Composer agrees to conduct and supervise at all music recording sessions.

   First Priority to Film: Composer agrees to give this project "first priority" during the term of this agreement and not expend substantial efforts on other composing work.

Disposition of Score: Producer reserves the right not to accept, use, or promote in any way the Score as provided by Composer. Producer reserves the right to request and Composer agrees to make such changes as Producer deems appropriate in the Score prior to delivery.

Delivery: Composer will deliver final music mix recordings as follows:

(a)   Producer will provide Composer with time code work tape containing the final edit ("locked" picture) no later than January 10, 1997.

(b)   Composer will prepare synthesizer demos of principal cues and themes for review by Producer no later than January 24, 1997. Producer agrees to provide any notes or corrections based on these demos to Composer no later than January 27, 1997.

(c)   Composer agrees to deliver final music mix recordings no later than February 10, 1997.

(d)   Producer to specify tape format and any other technical details for final music mix delivery.

Compensation: Producer agrees to a fee of $75,000, payable as follows:

$25,000   payable upon execution of this agreement or commencement of work, whichever comes first;
$25,000   payable upon commencement of recording sessions and
$25,000   payable upon completion of the recording sessions

All payments should be sent to Calvin Composer at the address included at the end of this agreement.

Screen Credit: Single Card Credit in the Main title of the picture on a separate card to read:

Music Composed and Conducted By
Calvin Composer

Size and placement at the Producer's discretion, however size to be no less favorable than that afforded the Director or Writer.

Music Publishing and Performing Rights Royalties: The music publishing company designated for the Score will be FredFilm Music Publishing (ASCAP). FredFilm Music Publishing will own 100% of all worldwide music publishing rights for the Score as described herein. Producer agrees to specify Calvin Composer (ASCAP) as 100% writer and FredFilm Music Publishing (ASCAP) as 100%

publisher for all music composed by Calvin Composer on performing rights cue sheets. Producer agrees to prepare accurate performing rights cue sheets and file with ASCAP and provide a copy to Composer no later than 30 days after the sound mix of the film

Ownership of Sound Recordings: The owner of the final sound recordings for all music used in the Film will be Fred Film Works. Fred Film Works will own 100% of all worldwide master rights to all music written by Calvin Composer used in the Film.

Rights of Producer: Composer acknowledges and agrees that Producer shall be deemed the author of the Score and shall own, and to the extent necessary to accomplish such ownership by Producer, Composer hereby sells, grants, assigns, and transfers to Producer, irrevocably, absolutely and throughout the entire universe, all rights of every kind, nature, and description in and to the Score, the results of Composer's services hereunder and the results of the services of all third parties rendering services in connection with the Score, together with all rights of every kind, nature and description in and to the title, words, music and performance of the Score and all copyrights therein and extensions and renewals of copyrights therein and all rights existing under all agreements and licenses relating thereto.

Originality and Copyright Considerations: Composer certifies that Composer composed the musical works described herein (the "Score") as an independent contractor engaged by Producer. Composer certifies that the Score is wholly original with Composer, except to the extent that it is based on or uses material in the public domain or material furnished to Composer by Producer, and that Producer is the author at law thereof and owns all right, title, and interest in and to the Score and the results of Composer's services rendered in connection therewith (all of which shall be considered as a "work-made-for-hire," specially commissioned by Producer as part of an audiovisual work), including without limitation all copyrights and renewals and extensions of copyrights therein.

Other Royalties: Producer agrees to pay to Composer, and Composer agrees to accept, the following royalties with respect to the Score:

(a)   Eight cents ($.08) per copy for each regular piano sheet music copy sold at wholesale in the United States, and not returned, and for which Producer is paid, which contains music or lyrics of the Score.

(b)   Ten Percent (10%) of the net wholesale selling price (after deduction of taxes and customary discounts) of each dance orchestration, folio, composite work or other printed publication (except regular piano sheet music copies) sold in the United States.

(c)   Fifty Percent (50%) of all net sums actually received by

Producer for regular piano copies, dance orchestrations, folios, composite works and other printed publications which contain music or lyrics of the Score, which are sold outside of the United States, and not returned.

(d) Fifty Percent (50%) of all net sums actually received by Producer for licensing of mechanical instrument, electrical transcription, motion picture and television synchronization, video cassette and disc recordings (other than soundtrack album(s) for the Film).

(e) Fifty Percent (50%) of any net recovery obtained and received by Producer as a result of any legal action brought by Producer against any alleged infringer of the Score after deduction of all expenses related to such legal action.

Producer shall not be required to account for or pay royalties on professional or complimentary copies and records (including compact discs, tape recordings and other embodiments of the Score), or copies and records distributed for promotional or charitable purposes.

Soundtrack and Song Compilation Album Royalties: Should Producer release or cause to be released any soundtrack albums containing music from the Film, Producer shall pay to Composer a royalty fee of 8% of the suggested retail price for each album sold for Composer's music as used on the album. All other aspects of soundtrack album creation and inclusion of Score on any soundtrack or song compilation albums subject to good faith negotiation.

Paid Advertising: Producer will make best efforts for composer credit, as set forth above, to appear in all advertisements for the film, including print, broadcast, and other forms of advertising. Size and placement at Producer's discretion, however in no case shall size and placement be less favorable than that afforded to the director or writer of the film.

Name and Likeness: Composer hereby grants to Producer the non-exclusive right in perpetuity to use and grant to others the right to use Composer's name and likeness in any and all media in connection with Composer's services under this Agreement.

Warranty and Certificate of Authorship: Composer represents and warrants to Producer that (i) Composer has full right and legal capacity to execute and fully perform this Agreement and to make the grants, assignments and waivers contained in it, (ii) that Composer warrants and confirms that he is the sole writer of the original musical compositions ("Score") delivered to Producer for use in the film and that the Score will not be copied from or based on, in whole or in part, any other work; (iii) to the best of Composer's knowledge as far as Composer knows or should have known in the exercise of due diligence and prudence, nothing in the Score does or will infringe on any property right (copyright, trademark, patent right, right to ideas and the like) or personal right (defamation, false light, moral right and the like) of any person or legal entity; and (iv) there is no pending or threatened claim, litigation, arbitration, action or proceeding with respect to the Score. Composer will indemnify and hold harmless Producer, its affiliated companies, successors and assigns, and their respective directors, employees and agents, from and against any claim, loss, liability, damages or judgements, including reasonable outside attorneys' fees, arising from any breach of the above representations and warranties.

This agreement will inure to the benefit of Producer's successors, assigns, lessees, and licensees. Composer will execute, acknowledge and deliver such additional instruments as necessary to confirm the intent of this Agreement.

This instrument is the entire Agreement between the parties and cannot be modified except by a written instrument signed by the Composer and an authorized officer of the Producer.

This Agreement shall be governed by and construed under and in accordance with the laws of the State of California applicable to agreements wholly performed therein.

Agreed to and accepted by the following parties on this _____ day of _____, 1997.

PRODUCER   **COMPOSER**

_____   _____
Fred Filmmaker   Calvin Composer
Fred Film Works, Inc.   2359 Santa Monica Boulevard #911
9999 Sunset Boulevard   Los Angeles, CA 90099
Suite 007
Los Angeles, CA 90099

ANALYSIS OF CONTRACT SECTIONS

Header and Introduction Section

January 1, 1997

Mr. Fred Filmmaker
Fred Film Works, Inc.
9999 Sunset Boulevard
Suite 007
Los Angeles, CA 90099

Dear Mr. Filmmaker:

Thanks for the opportunity to work with you on *Fred's Nightmare*. The following will outline the agreement between Fred Film Works, Inc. ("Producer") and
Calvin Composer ("Composer") in conjunction with the motion picture currently
entitled *Fred's Nightmare* ("Film").

This section defines who the agreement is between — in this example the agreement is between the composer and the film production company. If you operate your business as a corporation, you may want to structure the agreement so it is between your corporation and the filmmaker (consult your attorney for more information on this option). Many filmmakers, however, will insist that you be personally bound to the agreement because they consider this a personal services contract. Again, your attorney can provide legal guidance in this area.

Description of Services (Package Deal)

Services: Producer hereby engages Composer as an independent contractor to write, compose, arrange, adapt, score, orchestrate, produce, conduct, record, complete and deliver the instrumental score to be used in conjunction with the motion picture *Fred's Nightmare* (hereinafter called "Score") including all costs incurred in the creation, production and delivery of the music master recordings. The score will include all underscore and non-vocal source music under the direction and approval of Producer. The following costs are

---

excluded from the score package and are not subject to this agreement:

    (a)   Mag stock
    (b)   Licensing of music not composed by Calvin Composer
    (c)   Music Editor services (other than those contracted by composer)
    (d)   Vocalists requested by producer
    (e)   On-camera and/or "sidelining" musicians
    (f)   Re-use, New Use, and all Residual payments to musicians

Composer agrees to orchestrate, score, and conduct at all music recording sessions, supervise all scoring and music mixing sessions, arrange for studio time and copying, and arrange for such other services and elements as may be required in connection with the Score.

This section describes what you as a composer will deliver and what is and isn't included in the *package*. Many low budget feature films use these types of agreements, and often it is up to the composer to keep costs down because he/she is legally responsible for them as described in this section of the Composer Agreement. If a music editor is not supplied by the film company, the composer has the option to hire and pay for music editing services. If the score is being recorded non-union, you may want to omit item *(f)* above.

Description of Services (Non-Package Deal)

Services: Producer hereby engages Composer as an independent contractor to compose the score for *Fred's Nightmare* (hereinafter called "Score") including all underscore and non-vocal source music under the direction and approval of Producer.

Producer agrees to pay for all production costs incurred in the orchestration and recording of score including but not limited to the following:

    (a)   Orchestrator(s)
    (b)   Music Preparation Services (including copyists)
    (c)   Recording Costs (including musicians, applicable union benefits and payments, and all studio and recording session costs)
    (d)   Media Costs (including all tape costs and storage costs)
    (e)   Vocalists requested by producer
    (f)   On-camera and/or "sidelining" musicians

```
        (g)    Re-use, New Use, and all Residual payments to musicians

Producer reserves the exclusive right to choose, negotiate, and approve any
and all costs incurred in the orchestration and recording of the score.

Composer agrees to conduct and supervise at all music recording sessions.
```

This section describes what you as a composer will deliver and who is responsible for various costs incurred in the writing and recording of the music. Since there are many specific points and provisions that are unique to each project, we've only included the major points here. Your actual Composer Agreement should be as detailed as possible, listing all possible costs and contingencies and who will be responsible for payment and when they will be paid. You may also want to customize the language about who can approve certain choices, like the selection of a music editor, music preparation service, music contractor, or recording studio, depending on how your deal is structured with the client.

First Priority to Film

```
        First Priority to Film: Composer agrees to give this project "first
priority" during the term of this agreement and not expend substantial efforts
on other composing work.
```

This section obligates the composer to give this project *first priority* during the term of the agreement. Other than on very low budget films, this is standard language that most producers insist on.

Disposition of Score and Changes

```
        Disposition of Score: Producer reserves the right not to accept, use,
or promote in any way the Score as provided by Composer. Producer reserves
the right to request and Composer agrees to make such changes as Producer
deems appropriate in the Score prior to delivery.
```

This language covers situations where the Producer may choose to reject a score or request changes during the composing process. Most composers attempt to avoid wholesale rejections of their scores by working with the Producer to accommodate all requested changes during the composing, recording, and post production phases of the project.

Delivery Schedule

Delivery: Composer will deliver final music mix recordings as follows: Synthesizer demos with video will be provided for principal cues and themes during the period the music is being written. All final music will be delivered 4 weeks after receipt of the time code work tape containing the final edit ("locked" picture) from Producer. Producer to specify tape format and any other technical details for final music mix delivery.

The delivery schedule for your music is defined in this section. There are different ways to specify the critical dates in a project, including the language used above for when your time code work tape (*locked* picture) will be received on an undetermined date. If the time code work tape delivery date is known, the following language may be more appropriate:

Delivery: Composer will deliver final music mix recordings as follows:

(a) Producer will provide Composer with time code work tape containing the final edit ("locked" picture) no later than January 10, 1997.

(b) Composer will prepare synthesizer demos of principal cues and themes for review by Producer no later than January 24, 1997. Producer agrees to provide any notes or corrections based on these demos to Composer no later than January 27, 1997.

(c) Composer agrees to deliver final music mix recordings no later than February 10, 1997.

(d) Producer to specify tape format and any other technical details for final music mix delivery.

In some cases, especially where the filmmaker is making arrangements and/or paying for recording costs, you may want to include additional dates such as the date(s) for recording sessions and music mixing sessions.

Compensation

> **Compensation:** Producer agrees to a fee of $50,000, payable as follows:
>
> $25,000   payable upon execution of this agreement or commencement of work, whichever comes first;
>
> $12,500   payable upon commencement of recording sessions and
>
> $12,500   payable upon delivery of music master recordings
>
> All payments should be sent to Calvin Composer at the address included at the end of this agreement.

This section specifies who will receive payments, the amounts of the payments, and when they will be paid. You may want to specify dates rather than events, depending on your project.

There are also many clauses that your clients may want to include, such as non-performance ("if composer fails to perform certain tasks…"), sickness or injury, and crimes ("if composer is convicted of a felony during the course of the agreement…"). In general, these clauses often favor the client, so you may want to include them only if specifically requested. Often the client will provide specific language he/she wants included for these purposes. Any client-provided language should always be examined by your attorney.

Screen Credit

> **Screen Credit:** Single Card Credit in the Main title of the picture on a separate card to read:
>
> Music Composed and Conducted By
> Calvin Composer
>
> Size and placement at the Producer's discretion, however size to be no less favorable than that afforded the Director or Writer.

This is a standard part of *every* Composer Agreement. You may want to include additional language to provide for screen credit for your music editor, engineer, orchestrator(s), assistant(s), and others.

These credits are sometimes difficult to negotiate later if they're not included in the Composer Agreement. However, some filmmakers are reluctant to guarantee screen credit to any music personnel other than the composer(s). If possible, it is generally a good idea to include any credits you feel are absolutely necessary for key members of your music team.

Music Publishing (Composer Retains Publishing)

> **Music Publishing and Performing Rights Royalties:** The music publishing company designated for the Score will be CalvinWorks Publishing (ASCAP). CalvinWorks Publishing will own 100% of all worldwide music publishing rights for the Score as described herein. Producer agrees to specify Calvin Composer (ASCAP) as 100% writer and CalvinWorks Publishing (ASCAP) as 100% publisher for all music composed by Calvin Composer on performing rights cue sheets. Producer agrees to prepare accurate performing rights cue sheets and file with ASCAP and provide a copy to Composer and CalvinWorks Publishing no later than 30 days after the sound mix of the film.

This example specifies that the composer's publishing company will retain all ownership of the music used in the film. It also specifies how the performing rights cue sheets should be prepared and how you and your publishing company should be listed. In some cases, film production companies may not want to agree to a specific timetable for preparation of performing rights cue sheets. In this case, it is often best to agree to complete the cue sheets yourself or have it done by a music editor. Since you will be receiving 100% of the performing rights royalties, it is in your best interest to make sure the cue sheets are promptly prepared and filed.

Music Publishing (Producer Retains Publishing)

> **Music Publishing and Performing Rights Royalties:** The music publishing company designated for the Score will be FredFilm Music Publishing (ASCAP). FredFilm Music Publishing will own 100% of all worldwide music publishing rights for the Score as described herein. Producer agrees to specify Calvin Composer (ASCAP) as 100% writer and FredFilm Music Publishing (ASCAP) as 100% publisher for all music composed by Calvin Composer on performing rights cue sheets. Producer agrees to prepare accurate performing rights cue sheets and file with ASCAP and provide a copy to Composer no later than 30 days after the sound mix of the film. Producer agrees that all music provided by Composer that is rejected or not used in the final version of *Fred's Nightmare* shall remain the property of and 100% owned by composer.

Under this scenario the composer gives up all music publishing rights (which is essentially the ownership of the music) to the Client. This is not unusual for film scores written for medium to high budget projects and for television projects.

The last sentence allows you to retain all rights to rejected cues. This is a nice provision to include if you can, but keep in mind that some filmmakers will reject this. Also, a problematic situation can be created when this language is included and the filmmaker rejects a cue that contains a theme that is used in other parts of the film. You may want to include or expand this language based on the specifics of your project.

In addition to direct assignment of 100% of the publishing rights, some other methods exist for handling the ownership of music publishing rights, including the following:

Split Publishing	Under this type of arrangement the publishing rights are split between the composer and filmmaker. Both will share in any publishing revenue (future sync fees, mechanical royalties, sheet music and publisher's performing rights royalties).
Profit Participation	Sometimes a filmmaker will offer the composer a share of the future profits from a film as a way of reducing the initial composer fees. Since profit can be determined a number of different ways, you should always consult with an experienced entertainment attorney before entering into any sort of profit sharing arrangement.

Master Rights (Producer Retains Master Rights)

```
        Ownership of Sound Recordings: The owner of the final sound recordings
    for all music used in the Film will be Fred Film Works. Fred Film Works will
    own 100% of all worldwide master rights to all music written by Calvin
    Composer used in the Film.
```

This paragraph indicates that the producer will own all rights to the sound recordings of the music used in the film. As with publishing rights, the producer may want to have master rights ownership to all music written for the film, including rejected cues. Master rights become important when a composer wishes to release or have released a soundtrack album for the film, since whoever owns the master rights to the music essentially controls whether or not a soundtrack album can be made legally.

Rights / Work for Hire / Copyright Section (Producer Retains Publishing)

> **Rights of Producer:** Composer acknowledges and agrees that Producer shall be deemed the author of the Score and shall own, and to the extent necessary to accomplish such ownership by Producer, Composer hereby sells, grants, assigns, and transfers to Producer, irrevocably, absolutely and throughout the entire universe, all rights of every kind, nature, and description in and to the Score, the results of Composer's services hereunder and the results of the services of all third parties rendering services in connection with the Score, together with all rights of every kind, nature and description in and to the title, words, music and performance of the Score and all copyrights therein and extensions and renewals of copyrights therein and all rights existing under all agreements and licenses relating thereto.
>
> **Originality and Copyright Considerations:** Composer certifies that Composer composed the musical works described herein (the "Score") as an independent contractor engaged by Producer. Composer certifies that the Score is wholly original with Composer, except to the extent that it is based on or uses material in the public domain or material furnished to Composer by Producer, and that Producer is the author at law thereof and owns all right, title, and interest in and to the Score and the results of Composer's services rendered in connection therewith (all of which shall be considered as a "work-made-for-hire," specially commissioned by Producer as part of an audiovisual work), including without limitation all copyrights and renewals and extensions of copyrights therein.

This section is included when the Client retains publishing rights. Note that the language in this example would make the Composer responsible for all ownership issues should they arise with assistant composers, ghostwriters, or any other contributing third party.

If the composer retains the publishing and copyright on the score, then the language "...Producer is the author at law..." should be changed to "...Composer is the author at law...." Then delete the text "(all of which shall be considered as a "work-made-for-hire," specially commissioned by Producer as part of an audiovisual work)." See sample agreement #1 for an example of this section applicable to package deals where the composer retains publishing rights.

This text also specifies that the Producer is the copyright owner and has all rights to the music. This section will sometimes include further text that goes into detail about what kinds of rights are included, including the Producer's right to alter the music. This area should be carefully reviewed by you and your attorney to make sure that you and the Producer both agree on how the music can be used in the film and in any other related products such as sequels, the-making-of products, music videos for songs included in the film, and advertisements and trailers for other films the production company may produce now or in the future. These are all areas which can significantly affect you and the Producer in the future.

Other Royalties and Payments

Other Royalties: Producer agrees to pay to Composer, and Composer agrees to accept, the following royalties with respect to the Score:

(a)   Eight cents ($.08) per copy for each regular piano sheet music copy sold at wholesale in the United States, and not returned, and for which Producer is paid, which contains music or lyrics of the Score.

(b)   Ten Percent (10%) of the net wholesale selling price (after deduction of taxes and customary discounts) of each dance orchestration, folio, composite work or other printed publication (except regular piano sheet music copies) sold in the United States.

(c)   Fifty Percent (50%) of all net sums actually received by Producer for regular piano copies, dance orchestrations, folios, composite works and other printed publications which contain music or lyrics of the Score, which are sold outside of the United States, and not returned.

(d)   Fifty Percent (50%) of all net sums actually received by Producer for licensing of mechanical instrument, electrical transcription, motion picture and television synchronization, video cassette and disc recordings (other than soundtrack album(s) for the Film).

(e)   Fifty Percent (50%) of any net recovery obtained and received by Producer as a result of any legal action brought by Producer against any alleged infringer of the Score after deduction of all expenses related to such legal action.

Producer shall not be required to account for or pay royalties on professional or complimentary copies and records (including compact discs, tape recordings and other embodiments of the Score), or copies and records distributed for promotional or charitable purposes.

This language specifies additional royalties that may be paid if the music is exploited or distributed in different ways. The Producer may want to go into greater detail than what is presented in this example, but try to make any language in this area simple and clear, with a minimum number of exceptions. Also note that although the Producer may agree to pay certain royalties on sheet music or future Synchronization Licenses, most Composer Agreements will not obligate the Producer to exploit your music in any way. In fact, the film itself may not be released in certain cases. Note that soundtrack album royalties are excluded from this paragraph but are covered in separate language below.

IMPORTANT: The Producer may insist on including language that stipulates that the Composer will receive no payment if the music is used in other motion picture or television projects produced by Producer's company. This is a very delicate area and one that should be carefully negotiated. If the film is a success, there will inevitably be spin-off projects such as sequels, the-making-of projects, and television projects. Make sure the language in your agreement reflects your wishes as to if and when the Producer can use your music in *related projects* by his/her or other companies.

In general, when your music will be owned by the Client, make sure you understand the Client's intentions and plans for the film and your music. This should help avoid any misunderstandings later on.

Synchronization / Master Licenses (Composer Retains Publishing)

```
        Synchronization and Master Licenses for Score: Composer shall grant
Producer and its successors, assigns, and licenses the irrevocable right,
privilege and authority to record, copy, sell, distribute, and perform the
score subject to the terms of the Synchronization and Master Licenses sup-
plied with this document.
```

This language should only be used when the Composer retains some or all of the music publishing rights. The language provides that under the terms of the Synchronization and Master Use Licenses included in the Composer Agreement, the Client may use the music in the film. Without these licenses, the Client may not legally be able to use the music created under this agreement since the Composer retains all ownership, so this language and the accompanying Synchronization and Master Use Licenses are required when the Composer retains publishing rights.

Soundtrack or Song Compilation Album Royalties (Producer Retains Publishing)

> **Soundtrack and Song Compilation Album Royalties:** Should Producer release or cause to be released any soundtrack albums containing music from the Film, Producer shall pay to Composer a royalty fee of 8% of the suggested retail price for each album sold for Composer's music as used on the album. All other aspects of soundtrack album creation and inclusion of Score on any soundtrack or song compilation albums subject to good faith negotiation.

Usually when a soundtrack album is planned, there are a number of issues that need to be negotiated between the composer and the producer. These issues include the composer's royalties (usually 5 - 6% if the composer is not the producer, and 8 - 9% if the composer produces the album), the split of royalties when works from multiple composers are included on an album (usually split proportionally by minutes of music or number of cues), and soundtrack album credits. Each soundtrack album deal is different and can involve multiple parties, such as the Producer, a record company, and the distributor of the film. This is an area where consulting an *experienced entertainment attorney is highly recommended.*

Paid Advertising and Promotion, Name and Likeness

> **Paid Advertising:** Producer will make best efforts for composer credit, as set forth above, to appear in all advertisements for the film, including print, broadcast, and other forms of advertising. Size and placement at Producer's discretion, however in no case shall size and placement be less favorable than that afforded to the director or writer of the film.
>
> **Name and Likeness:** Composer hereby grants to Producer the non-exclusive right in perpetuity to use and grant to others the right to use Composer's name and likeness in any and all media in connection with Composer's services under this Agreement.

This language obligates the Producer (but makes no guarantee) to include the Composer's name and credit ("music composed and conducted by") in paid advertising for the film including posters, trailers, television advertisements, etc. Some filmmakers will be reluctant to approve this language as advertising may be not 100% controlled by them. Also, it is common with low budget films to prepare some of the print advertising before a composer is even hired. The *best efforts* language is often acceptable to a Producer as it indicates an intention but is not a guarantee.

The *Name and Likeness* allows the Producer to use your name and likeness (which usually includes such things as your picture and biography) in advertising for the film, and protects the Producer against claims by you that you did not give permission for the Producer to use your name and likeness. Note that if you agree to this clause, you may not be able to remove your name from advertising and screen credit for the film should you decide you wish to do this in the future.

Warranty / Certificate of Authorship

> **Warranty and Certificate of Authorship:** Composer represents and warrants to Producer that (i) Composer has full right and legal capacity to execute and fully perform this Agreement and to make the grants, assignments and waivers contained in it, (ii) that Composer warrants and confirms that he is the sole writer of the original musical compositions ("Score") delivered to Producer for use in the film and that the Score will not be copied from or based on, in whole or in part, any other work; (iii) to the best of Composer's knowledge as far as Composer knows or should have known in the exercise of due diligence and prudence, nothing in the Score does or will infringe on any property right (copyright, trademark, patent right, right to ideas and the like) or personal right (defamation, false light, moral right and the like) of any person or legal entity; and (iv) there is no pending or threatened claim, litigation, arbitration, action or proceeding with respect to the Score. Composer will indemnify and hold harmless Producer, its affiliated companies, successors and assigns, and their respective directors, employees and agents, from and against any claim, loss, liability, damages or judgements, including reasonable outside attorneys' fees, arising from any breach of the above representations and warranties.

This is standard, required text in almost all Composer Agreements, and is intended to protect the Producer from various claims of copyright infringement, plagiarism, copying, theft of ideas, or other damages. This language is sometimes carefully inspected by the Producer's insurance company who often protects this area of the Producer's business with an *Errors and Omissions* insurance policy.

Final Notes and Terms

This agreement will inure to the benefit of Producer's successors, assigns, lessees, and licensees. Composer will execute, acknowledge and deliver such additional instruments as necessary to confirm the intent of this Agreement.

This instrument is the entire Agreement between the parties and cannot be modified except by a written instrument signed by the Composer and an authorized officer of the Producer.

This Agreement shall be governed by and construed under and in accordance with the laws of the State of California applicable to agreements wholly performed therein.

Agreed to and accepted by the following parties on this _____ day of _____, 1997.

PRODUCER

_____

Fred Filmmaker
Fred Film Works, Inc.
9999 Sunset Boulevard
Suite 007
Los Angeles, CA 90099

COMPOSER

_____

Calvin Composer
2359 Santa Monica Boulevard #911
Los Angeles, CA 90099

This final section contains language that specifies that the agreement will continue to be in force with anyone the Producer decides to transfer or sell the agreement to, that it is the entire agreement between the composer and Producer, and that it will be governed by the laws of the state of California.

SYNCHRONIZATION LICENSE

Prepared By   Composer, Agent, Manager, or Composer's Attorney

When to Use   When a filmmaker wants to use music you own in a film or television project. The Synchronization license gives the filmmaker the right to use or record your music in relation to his/her picture. You may also need to issue a Master License if the filmmaker wishes to use your recording of the music (see next section).

Description   A Synchronization License (or Sync License) is granted by the owner or publisher of a piece of music and allows the music to be used or recorded in timed-relation with a picture.

If you have a Composer Agreement where you retain the publishing, you will need to include a sync license (and possibly a Master Use License) as part of the Composer Agreement. This will allow the filmmaker to use your music in his/her film. Note that a sync license only gives permission to use <u>the music</u>. Permission to use a <u>specific recording of the music</u>, which is typical unless the client wants to re-record the music himself, is usually covered by a Master Use License (see next section).

Note that this example assumes the Synchronization License is provided as part of an overall Composer Agreement, and that composer fees are included in the agreement. The inclusion of "$1.00 and other good and valuable consideration" language is necessary to make the license an agreement with *consideration* (something of value given/received) between the parties.

If you are issuing a Synchronization License which is not part of the original Composer Agreement (such as when you license music you own for other projects), you should adjust the fee language appropriately and have both yourself and the producer sign the license.

SCORE SYNCHRONIZATION LICENSE

For and in consideration of Producer's agreement to pay a license fee in the sum of $1 and other good and valuable consideration to the undersigned publisher (CalvinWorks Publishing (ASCAP) "Publisher"), Publisher hereby grants to the producer, Fred Film Works, Inc., and its successors, assigns, and licenses (herein referred to as "Producer"), the exclusive, irrevocable right, license, privilege and authority to:

(a)   Record the musical composition identified below (including the music and/or lyrics thereof in any arrangement, orchestration or language), but only in the synchronization or timed relation with the motion picture identified below;

(b)   Make any number of copies of said recordings;

(c)   Sell, license, distribute, subdistribute, export, and import said recordings and/or copies from and into any country or territory throughout the universe; and

(d)   Perform said musical composition throughout the universe but only in synchronization or timed relation with the motion picture identified below, upon and subject to the terms and conditions set forth below:

1.   The musical composition covered by this license is:
     Composition: *Fred's Nightmare* (all score music)
     Publishers share: 100% world

2.   The present working title of the motion picture with which said recording will be used is *Fred's Nightmare*. As used herein, the term "motion picture" refers to said motion picture and all versions thereof now or hereafter in existence, whether in English or foreign language, television, or any other form, (but not including remakes or sequels), and trailers, promotional films, television and radio spots, clips and excerpts of said motion picture or any version thereof.

3.   The territory covered by this license is the universe.

4.   The music publishing company designated for the musical composition will be CalvinWorks Publishing (ASCAP). CalvinWorks Publishing will own 100% of all worldwide music publishing rights for the Score as described herein. Producer agrees to specify Calvin Composer (ASCAP) as 100% writer and CalvinWorks Publishing (ASCAP) as 100% publisher for all music composed by Calvin Composer on performing rights cue sheets. Producer agrees to prepare accurate performing rights cue sheets and file with ASCAP and provide a copy to Composer no later than 30 days after the sound mix of the film.

5.   This license shall remain in full force and effect for the duration of all copyrights in said musical composition, including any renewals and extensions without Producer having to pay any additional consideration thereof.

6.   The recording rights granted in (a) above may be exercised by any and all means, methods, and systems of recording sound in synchronization or timed relation with motion pictures, whether now known or hereafter devised.

"Fred's Nightmare" Score Synchronization License
Page 2

7.   Publisher warrants that it has the right to grant this license, that it owns and controls one hundred percent (100%) of the right, title and interest in and to said musical composition and that the use of said musical composition hereunder will not violate the rights of any third party. Publisher shall indemnify costs, losses, damages and expenses (including reasonable attorneys fees) arising out of any breach or failure of any warranties or covenants made by Publisher herein.

8.   Subject only to the rights herein above granted to Producer, all rights of every kind and nature in said musical compositions are reserved to said Publisher, together with all rights of use thereof. However, in no event shall Producer have less rights than a member of the public would have in the absence of this license.

9.   No failure by Producer to perform any of its obligations hereunder shall constitute a breach of this license, unless Publisher has given Producer written notice of such non-performance and producer fails to cure such non-performance within thirty (30) days of its receipt of such notice.

10. Publisher's rights and remedies in the event of a breach of this license shall be limited to Publisher's right, if any, to recover damages in an action at law.

11. Producer agrees to give credit to the composer, full card in the main titles to read:

Music Composed and Conducted By
Calvin Composer

12. Producer agrees not to manufacture or distribute sound recordings (including soundtrack albums, promotional CDs, and any and all methods of sound recording) separately from actual positive prints of the motion picture and directly integrated media (such as digital recordings to be used in theaters as part of a theater's digital sound reproduction system).

13. This license shall be governed by and subject to the laws of the State of California applicable to agreements made and to be wholly performed therein.

14. This license is binding upon and shall inure to the benefit of the respective successors and/or assigns of the parties hereto.

15. This represents the entire agreement between Producer and Publisher with regard to said musical composition.

MASTER USE LICENSE

Prepared By   Composer, Agent, Manager, or Composer's Attorney

When to Use   When a filmmaker wants to use a specific recording of music owned by you in a film or television project. It is almost always used in conjunction with a Synchronization License (see previous section).

Description   A Master Use License is granted by the owner of a sound recording (usually the author of the song or a record company if the sound recording is part of a commercial album) and allows the use of that <u>specific recording</u> of the music in a film or television project.

With some exceptions, such as Public Domain compositions, a Master Use License usually requires an accompanying Synchronization License. Note that if the music publishing and sound recordings are owned by different entities, the filmmaker may find himself negotiating separately for each license.

If the sound recording in the Master Use License was recorded by Union Musicians then you should advise the filmmaker that he/she will need to check with the AF of M to see if any additional payments will need to be made to the musicians who originally played on the recording.

SCORE MASTER USE LICENSE

For and in consideration of Producer's agreement to pay a license fee in the sum of $1 and other good and valuable consideration to CalvinWorks, CalvinWorks hereby grants to the producer, Fred Film Works, Inc., and its successors, assigns, and licenses (herein referred to as "Producer"), the exclusive, irrevocable right, license, privilege and authority to use specified Recording as follows:

1.   The musical recording covered by this license is:

        Recording: Musical composition *Fred's Nightmare* (all score music) ("Recording")

        CalvinWorks' share: 100% world

2.   The present working title of the motion picture with which said recording will be used is *Fred's Nightmare*. As used herein, the term "motion picture" refers to said motion picture and all versions thereof now or hereafter in existence, whether in English or foreign language, television, or any other form, (but not including remakes or sequels), and trailers, promotional films, television and radio spots, clips and excerpts of said motion picture or any version thereof.

3.   The territory covered by this license is the universe.

4.   This license shall remain in full force and effect for the duration of all copyrights in said musical composition, including any renewals and extensions without Producer having to pay any additional consideration thereof.

5.   CalvinWorks warrants that it has the right to grant this license, that it owns and controls one hundred percent (100%) of the right, title and interest in and to Recording and that the use of said Recording hereunder will not violate the rights of any third party. CalvinWorks shall indemnify costs, losses, damages and expenses (including reasonable attorneys fees) arising out of any breach or failure of any warranties or covenants made by CalvinWorks herein.

6.   Subject only to the rights herein above granted to Producer, all rights of every kind and nature in said Recording are reserved to CalvinWorks, together with all rights of use thereof. However, in no event shall Producer have less rights than a member of the public would have in the absence of this license.

7.   No failure by Producer to perform any of its obligations hereunder shall constitute a breach of this license, unless CalvinWorks has given Producer written notice of such non-performance and producer fails to cure such non-performance within thirty (30) days of its receipt of such notice.

8.   CalvinWorks' rights and remedies in the event of a breach of this license shall be limited to CalvinWorks' right, if any, to recover damages in an action at law.

"Fred's Nightmare" Score Master Use License
Page 2

9.   Producer agrees not to manufacture or distribute sound recordings (including soundtrack albums, promotional CDs, and any and all methods of sound recording) separately from actual positive prints of the motion picture and directly integrated media (such as digital recordings to be used in theaters as part of a theater digital sound reproduction system).

10.   Producer agrees to obtain all synchronization licenses necessary to utilizes the musical compositions embodied in the Recording in the soundtrack of the Film and any related entertainment products such as promotional films and advertisements.

11.   Producer agrees to pay all musicians' re-use, new-use, and all residual payments of any kind related to this use of the Recording.

12.   This license shall be governed by and subject to the laws of the State of California applicable to agreements made and to be wholly performed therein.

13.   This license is binding upon and shall inure to the benefit of the respective successors and/or assigns of the parties hereto.

14.   This represents the entire agreement between Producer and CalvinWorks with regard to Recording of said musical composition.

SYNC USE QUOTE REQUEST LETTER
MASTER USE QUOTE REQUEST LETTER

Prepared By   Filmmaker, Music Supervisor, or Composer

When to Use   This type of letter is used when a person wishes to license a piece of music or song and wants to get information on what fees would be charged for a specific type of use (e.g. film or television program)

Description   A Sync Use quote request letter or Master Use quote request letter is useful if you need to get quotes for using songs or score from <u>other</u> composers or songwriters. Once you have received rate information from the publishing company (for sync rights) or the record company (for master rights) you may want to enlist the services of a Music Supervisor to handle the negotiations and actual licensing of the music.

The process of negotiating and securing Synchronization and Master Use Licenses is also known as *clearing* music for use in film or television projects.

More information on clearing music can be found in Section IV of this Resource Guide under the title **Music Clearance for Songs and Source Music** in Section IV. The ASCAP Internet site located at **http://www.ascap.com** also has excellent information on clearing songs and scores.

Sample Sync Use Quote Request Letter

Sally Supervisor
2359 Santa Monica Boulevard #911
Los Angeles, CA 90099
(310) 555-2368

SYNC USE QUOTE REQUEST

January 1, 1997   <u>VIA FACSIMILE</u>

To: Mr. Paul Publisher / Paul's House of Songs
From: Sally Supervisor
Re: *Fred's Nightmare* (Picture Title) — "Falling" (Song Title)

     We would like to obtain a quote for synchronization of the Sam
Songwriter composition "Falling" in conjunction with the above-titled
film. The details are as follows:

Title: "Falling"

Writer(s):   Sam Songwriter

Territory: The World

Term: Perpetuity, All Media Present and Hereafter Devised,
                Video, In-context trailers

Nature of use: Background source, total time not more than four
                minutes (4:00). The song would be played during a
                dream sequence. The main character, Fred, is having a
                nightmare about falling from a plane. The total time
                of the song would not exceed four minutes (4:00).

Director: Fred Filmmaker

Cast: Amy Actress, Adam Actor

Synopsis: A dark comedy about a young man's battle with
                nightmares of falling. Distributed by DD Distributing.

Should you have any questions, please call.

Sincerely,

Sally Supervisor

Sample Master Use Quote Request Letter

Sally Supervisor
2359 Santa Monica Boulevard #911
Los Angeles, CA 90099
(310) 555-2368

MASTER USE QUOTE REQUEST

January 1, 1997   <u>VIA FACSIMILE</u>

To: Mr. Ron Recorder / Ron's Record Company
From: Sally Supervisor
Re: *Fred's Nightmare* (Picture Title) - "Falling" (Song Title)

   We would like to obtain a quote for use of your master recording of Steve Singer performing the Sam Songwriter composition "Falling" in conjunction with the above-titled film. The details are as follows:

Title: "Falling" as performed by Steve Singer (1978)

Writer(s):   Sam Songwriter

Territory: The World

Term: Perpetuity, All Media Present and Hereafter Devised, Video, In-context trailer

Nature of use: Background source, total time not more than four minutes (4:00). The song would be played during a dream sequence. The main character, Fred, is having a nightmare about falling from a plane. The total time of the song would not exceed four minutes (4:00).

Director: Fred Filmmaker

Cast: Amy Actress, Adam Actor

Synopsis: A dark comedy about a young man's battle with nightmares of falling. Distributed by DD Distributing.

Should you have any questions, please call.

Sincerely,

Sally Supervisor

INDEPENDENT CONTRACTOR AGREEMENT FOR MUSICIANS

Prepared By   Composer or Composer's Assistant

When to Use   When hiring musicians as independent contractors

Description   This form serves to clarify a musician's working relationship with you as an independent contractor. You should ask your accountant or tax attorney to give you specific legal advice about this issue because the subject of whether musicians should be considered independent contractors or employees (for tax purposes) has a long history of debate.

This document simply asks the musician to state that he/she is an independent contractor, is responsible for paying his/her own taxes, and expects to receive no future revenues or fees for his/her work. You may want to delete the section about future payments if you are hiring the musician on some sort of royalty or future/deferred payment deal.

It is important to note that this document in no way protects you if the IRS decides to reclassify your independent contractors as employees (hire a good accountant if this seems likely!) but may at least clarify your intended relationship with the musicians.

Sample Independent Contractor Agreement for Musicians

**CINEMATRAX
INDEPENDENT CONTRACTOR AGREEMENT**

Name and Address:

Mary Musician

1000 Apple Lane

Los Angeles, 90068

(213) 555-1449

Social Security Number / Tax ID: *007-00-1000*

I understand and agree that my relationship with Cinematrax and/or Mark Northam/Lisa Anne Miller will be that of an independent contractor and not an employee. I am responsible for any and all taxes assessed with respect to compensation paid to me by Cinematrax. I understand that I will receive no residual payments or additional payments or benefits of any kind other than my direct pay for the recording sessions.

Signed *Mary Musician* Date: *May 1, 1996*

SECTION IV
OTHER COMPOSER RESOURCES

This section contains a wide variety of resources for film and television composers. Here you will find definitions of terms used in the business, current rates, examples of places that use original music and where to go for additional information. We've also included a special section on ASCAP, BMI, and SESAC because of the importance of composer revenue from these performing rights organizations, and for those interested, we've provided some basic information on music clearance.

Included in this section are:

Glossary of Film and Television Music Terms — This is a handy guide to various legal and technical terms used in the business, as well as descriptions of the most common film and television music professions.

Music Editor Terms and Abbreviations — Here are some of the specialized terms and abbreviations that music editors use in spotting and breakdown notes. Also used by directors and others describing camera shots, camera moves and picture edits.

An Introduction to ASCAP, BMI, and SESAC — Here the basics of Performing Rights Organizations are described. You may want to contact ASCAP, BMI, or SESAC directly for more detailed information. Contact information is listed in the **Organizations** section.

Music Clearance for Songs and Source Music — This is an introduction to the process of music licensing. For more information, consider contacting a music supervisor or attorney.

Current Rates — This is a very informal listing of current rates for composers, musicians, music editors, contractors, orchestrators, engineers and assistants in the Los Angeles market. We've compiled this list based on our experience and the experience of other film and television composers working in Los Angeles today. Please keep in mind, however, that this list is only an example. You may find rates for your type of work in your geographical area to be higher or lower than those listed here.

Fifty Places and Uses for Original Music — We included this as an example of different markets that use original music. You may want to use this list as a starting point when developing your marketing plan. It also may help you think of other people that may be interested in your music.

Schools That Offer Programs in Music for Film And Television — This is a list of colleges and schools that offer various programs and degrees in the study of film and television music.

Film and Television Music Agents — Here are some of the agents representing film and television music composers. We've included Los Angeles area agents primarily since that's where the majority of work is today.

Film and Television Music Attorneys — A list of attorneys that specialize in entertainment law in the Los Angeles area.

Organizations — This is a list of organizations that are directly or indirectly related to music for film and television.

Books — Here are some books we recommend for further study about the history, business, art, and craft of film and television scoring.

Magazines and Periodicals — We've included some important sources of weekly and daily information on the film and television music business. Note that some of these publications may be regional.

Computer Hardware and Software — This is an introduction to some of the software and hardware used for film and television music scoring. This is not a complete list, but may be handy as a starting point as you investigate what kinds of computer hardware and software to purchase for your studio.

Internet Resources — This is a list of some of our favorite Internet web sites and resources related to film and television music. Since the Internet changes and expands on a daily basis, this list can change or become outdated very quickly. We've included Internet resources that are operating as of this guide's publication.

GUIDE TO FILM AND TELEVISION MUSIC TERMS

This list contains many commonly used terms and job titles in the film and television music industry. Where *U.S.* is indicated after a term, the description applies to how the term is used in the United States. A term or reference may have a different meaning in countries other than the United States.

A F of M (American Federation of Musicians) (also known as the *Musicians Union*) — In the United States, this is the national Musicians Union. They have contract agreements with film and television production companies which cover the performance of their musician, orchestrator, and copyist members on recording sessions for film and television scores. The A F of M also oversees contracts for musicians working in live performances, album recording, demo recording, and radio and television jingles and commercials.

Answer Print — The first print of a film that is made after the negatives have been cut (edited).

Arranger — An arranger works with existing musical material and creates a custom version for a specific kind or size of musical group. For example, an arranger might be asked to take a piece of film music originally written for a large orchestra and create a version for a smaller musical group. Arrangers can also create versions of music in different styles, like arranging traditional music for a contemporary music group such as a big band or rock group.

ADR (Automated Dialogue Replacement) (or *Looping*) — The process of replacing dialogue lines in the original *production* audio tracks (the audio tracks recorded as the scene was filmed) with new recordings of the actor(s) reading the dialogue.

ASCAP — ASCAP stands for the American Society of Composers, Arrangers, and Publishers. ASCAP is a performing rights organization headquartered in the United States which administers the performing rights of its songwriter and composer members. ASCAP collects performance royalties from various sources including radio and television stations and networks, nightclubs, and live performances such as concerts. These royalties are distributed to its members based on how often their compositions are performed. Performing rights royalties are made up of two equal amounts called *Writer Royalties* and *Publishing Royalties*.

Assumption Agreement (U.S.) — An agreement that a production company must sign with the A F of M (Musicians Union) in order to use the services of union members on a film or television music recording session. The agreement covers various issues including who is responsible for paying potential future payments to the musicians based on any new uses of the music. The agreement also specifies any special payments to the musicians that may be required in the future based on the commercial success of the film.

BMI — BMI stands for Broadcast Music Incorporated and is a performing rights organization headquartered in the United States which administers the performing rights of its songwriter and composer members. BMI collects performance royalties from various sources including radio and television stations and networks, nightclubs, and live performances. These royalties are distributed to its members based on how often their compositions are performed. As with other performing rights organizations, BMI performing rights royalties are made up of two equal amounts called *Writer Royalties* and *Publishing Royalties*.

Breakdown Notes (or *Timing Notes*) — A document prepared by the Music Editor for a film or television production which details specific events within a scene. Breakdown Notes are almost always prepared by the Music Editor and are supplied in printed and electronic form, if requested, to the composer who uses these notes to reference the time code locations of events within a scene. Breakdown Notes usually contain the time code location of each event along with a brief description of the event. Most Breakdown Notes contain all camera moves and edits as well as key action and dialogue points. An example of Breakdown Notes is shown in section II of this Guide.

Bumper — A short piece of music that is played before or after a commercial or other break in a television program. The music signifies the beginning or end of a segment of the program.

Buy-out — A term used to describe a deal or arrangement where no future royalties or income will be paid to the person being hired. This term is sometimes used when a musician is hired for a non-union recording session and will not be paid any residuals or future payments.

Cartage — Fees charged by musicians to cover the cost of transporting certain large instruments such as keyboards, timpani, and other large equipment or instruments. Although there are scale cartage rates specified by the Musicians Union, most musicians negotiate their own rates based on their specific equipment and instruments.

Click (or *Click Track*) — Click is an audible metronome signal that the conductor and musicians hear through their headphones during recording. Click helps the conductor and musicians perform music at exactly the right tempo so that it will synchronize with the picture as the composer intended. Composers will either indicate a constant or varying click speed for each piece of music that is written. If the microphones inadvertently pick up this sound coming from the headphones during recording, the problem is called *click bleed*. Clicks that are played for musicians before the cue starts in order to establish the tempo of the cue are called *free clicks*.

Composer Agreement — The agreement between a film or television production company and a composer. The Composer Agreement often specifies the amount of music to be written, the tape format for delivery, the composer's compensation, and timetables for payment and delivery.

Conductor — The person who directs the musicians (usually from a podium) as they perform a piece of music. The conductor is often the person who composed or orchestrated the music. The conductor is often the only person in the recording room who can hear the comments of the people in the *booth* (control room) at a recording session. The Conductor listens to the comments and requests of the people in the control room and translates them into musical directions for the musicians.

Contractor — A contractor works with the composer for a film or television project to hire the musicians who will play on the recording sessions. The contractor also interfaces with the A F of M (Musicians Union) when appropriate to ensure that the proper paperwork and forms are completed and filed for union recording sessions. A good contractor also knows how to hire skilled, professional musicians, how to work with the musicians to ensure that the composer's needs are met, and knows how to hire musicians who work well together. The contractor is usually hired or designated by the composer.

Copyist (or *Music Preparation*) — A copyist performs services known as Music Preparation. These services include taking the printed scores prepared by the composer or orchestrator, which have separate lines for each instrument in the group to be recorded, and preparing individual parts (printed music sheets) for each musician. The copyist is responsible for making sure that the parts for the musicians are readable and contain exactly what is indicated in the printed score. Copyists often attend the recording sessions to make sure the parts are correctly distributed to the musicians and to make any last-minute changes to the score and parts that may be necessary before or during the recording session.

Cue — A piece of music written for a film or television project. Cues can be of any length and are written for a particular scene or scenes in a film. Cues can be *Score* cues (background or theme music) or *Source* cues (music that is heard by the actors in the scene, such as music in a nightclub or music coming out of a radio). Source cues are often music that already exists (such as songs from an album) that are licensed for use in a film. The Music Supervisor typically handles the licensing of source cues. *Cue* is also the name of a Macintosh computer music software package that allows input and printing of spotting and breakdown notes and handles most music editing tasks.

Cue Sheet (or _Performing Rights Cue Sheet_) — The document prepared after a film or television project is completed that specifies information about each cue and how it was used. The cue sheet indicates the composer, publishing company, performing rights affiliations of composer(s) and publisher(s), title, length as actually used, and usage (background instrumental, visual vocal, etc.) for each cue. This document is filed with the performing rights organizations (ASCAP, BMI, SESAC) that the composer(s) and publisher(s) are affiliated with, and is the basis for payment of performing rights royalties. The Cue Sheet is usually prepared by the Music Editor. Payment of performing rights royalties is only possible if a cue sheet is filed for a production.

Doubles — Instruments that a musician plays in addition to the their primary instrument. For example, a woodwind player may be hired to play flute, but also may double on the clarinet and piccolo. When a musicians plays doubles, he/she is usually compensated with additional pay. If recording under a union contract, the union has specified additional payment rates for doubles.

Dry — Refers to a track of music on tape that is recorded or played back without any electronic reverb, delay, or echo of any kind.

Dubbing Sheets — Reports that are prepared by the Music Editor for use at a dubbing (sound mixing) session. These sheets detail what music cues are on the music tapes from the composer, time code locations for the beginning and end of each cue, and which tracks of the tape are used for each cue. An example of a dubbing sheet is shown in section II of this Guide.

Engineer (see _Scoring Mixer_)

Final Cut (see _Locked Picture_)

Foley — Recorded movement of sounds that are recorded separately and then synchronized with picture. Foley is needed because certain sounds like footsteps and walking sounds are usually not recorded well (or are sometimes not recorded at all) in the production audio tracks. Foley is the process of recording movement sounds for synchronization to existing picture.

Free-time — Used to describe the process of recording music without a click track. The conductor references some other source such as a clock or events in the picture, and may use _streamers_ and *punches* added to the picture image to establish the correct timing of the music.

Ghostwriter — A person who composes music for another composer but is not credited on the cue sheet or in the final product in any way. In a ghostwriting situation, the person hiring the ghostwriter takes credit for writing the music and the ghostwriter is usually not allowed to reveal to anyone that he/she wrote the music or worked on the project in any way. Ghostwriting is one of the *dirty little secrets* of the film and television music business and is considered by most professional composers to be unethical.

Hummer — A derogatory term for someone who calls himself a *composer* but lacks the skills and knowledge to create an actual score synchronized to picture. Hummers usually achieve an image of success by taking credit for the products of others. Hummers require the assistance of many other composers, arrangers and orchestrators who are exploited and taken advantage of.   See also *Ghostwriter*.

Letterbox — A version of a film that is shown using its original rectangular dimensions . Non-letterbox versions of films are often edited to fit a television format, and visual material on the left and right sides of the picture may be lost. On letterbox editions of films, the film is seen in a rectangle on the television screen with black areas above and below the picture.

Librarian (or *Music Librarian*) — The person at a recording session who distributes and collects the printed music parts and conductor's score. This is often a function of the copyist or music preparation company.

Library Music (or *Production Music*) — A collection of music, usually available on CD, that can be licensed for use in a film or television project. Different payment options are available, including buy-outs where the production company pays a single fee for use of the music, and fees based on how much and how often the music is used.

Locked Picture — A film or television project is considered to be locked when all edits that could affect the timing of the picture are completed. The last edit of a film is sometimes called the final cut. If a composer is working with a locked picture, he/she can be confident that any synchronization of music to picture based on the locked picture will work with the final copy of the picture as long as he/she is working with the proper time code.

Master Rights — Refers to the privilege of using a specific existing sound recording of a piece of music in a film or television project. The owner of the sound recording (the *master*) must agree to allow the use of the recording in order for it to be used in a film or television project. A license to use an existing sound recording in a film or television project is called a Master Use License. An example of a Master Use License is shown in section III of this Guide.

MIDI — Musical Instrument Digital Interface. This is the language that computers, synthesizers, samplers, and other electronic musical instruments use to communicate with each other.

Most Favored Nations — Refers to a specific phrase which can be included as language in a sync or master use license. It essentially means: "This is my price and terms unless you give another company in my position a better deal. If you do, you agree to automatically revise my price and terms to be equal to the better price and terms." This language is often requested by publishers or recording companies when you are negotiating with more than one company or publisher on a project. Each company wants to make sure they get as favorable prices and terms as are being given to others for the project.

Music Clearance (or *Rights Licensing*) — Music Clearance refers to the negotiation of rights to use an existing song or piece of music in a film or television project. Usually the Music Supervisor handles the music clearance or *rights licensing* and works with the companies or individuals who have publishing rights (ownership of the music) and master rights (ownership of a sound recording of the music).

Music Editor — The Music Editor works with the composer and production company to organize, document, and time the music cues for a project. The Music Editor works very closely with the composer during the early phases of a production to document the decisions of the director and composer about the placement, timing, length, and type of music to be used throughout a project. The Music Editor is usually present during the recording sessions to document each cue as it is recorded, and may be responsible for generating the *click* that is often used to keep the timings of the performance precise (see *click*). The Music Editor is also present at the dubbing or prelay sessions where the recorded music is inserted into the film at the correct time code locations.

Music Supervisor — An executive who manages the licensing of music for a film or television production. The Music Supervisor handles music clearance and rights licensing of existing music, and also may be involved with supervising the score composer. Choosing appropriate music, especially Source Cues and Songs is usually the responsibility of the Music Supervisor.

Music Units — Generally refers to reels of tape containing final music. This term is used during dubbing sessions to refer to the source tapes containing music.

Opticals — A term that refers to any visual effect, including dissolves, fades, and wipes. Also refers to special effects such as computer generated images (CGI) or electronically created environments such as outer space.

Orchestrator — An Orchestrator takes the printed music from the composer (usually a semi-detailed score or less-detailed sketch) and makes decisions on which instruments will play various musical parts. The orchestrator then creates a detailed score that contains a single line for each instrument in the musical group or orchestra. This detailed score is supplied to the copyist who creates a single printed part from each line in the score for the musicians to play. The Orchestrator is often the orchestra conductor during recording sessions.

Performing Rights Royalties (U.S.) — Royalties that are charged for the public performance of music, including music used in television programs, bars and restaurants, and non-U.S. theaters. These royalties are collected by performing rights organizations (in the United States by ASCAP, BMI, and SESAC), and are paid to the songwriter, composer, and publisher members of these organizations based on various factors including how often the music is played and the historical popularity of the music.

Postscoring — Creating music for a film or television project <u>after</u> a picture has been filmed. This is the most common scenario for film scoring, and is the reason why music for film trailers (previews of coming attractions) and advertisements is often not from the actual film being advertised. Advertisements and trailers are often prepared long before the shooting, editing, and scoring phases of a film have been completed.

Prelay (or *Prelay Session, Layback Session*) — Refers to the process of *laying in* or recording music and other sound elements of a film or television project at the correct time code locations on a master format without regard to final levels and mixing. Once the prelay session is complete, the relative levels of the music, dialogue, ambiences and sound effects can be determined during the dubbing session. Today, the entire prelay and dub process is often done in a digital environment and is only recorded to tape after the entire project is mixed and completed.

Prerecord — Recording of music that is used during the shooting of a film or television project. The music must be recorded before the actual scene is filmed, since the actors in a scene must be able to synchronize their actions and movements to the music that will be used in the scene. Examples include dance scenes and scenes where the actor must sing or play an instrument.

Prescoring — Creating music for a film or television project <u>before</u> a picture has been filmed. The musical ideas are often based on ideas communicated by the director, the script, and specifications such as the length of the cues. Prescoring is very common in animation projects where the music and lyrics are recorded in the early part of a project. The animators then create drawings that synchronize with the recorded music.

Post Production — Refers to all activities in creating a film or television production that occur after the shooting ends. Examples of post production tasks include editing, adding sound effects and music, special visual/optical effects, and replacement of dialogue lines (also known as looping or ADR). Creating an original music score is almost always part of the post production phase of a film or television production.

Public Domain (PD) Composition — A composition that is no longer owned by a Publishing company (usually because of the amount of time that has passed since the composer has died) is said to be *in the Public Domain* and can be re-recorded without payment to a publisher or negotiation of rights. Note that existing recordings of public domain music may generally not be used without the permission of the owner of the recording. For example, a piece by Beethoven would be considered Public Domain, however, in order to be used in a film or television project a sound recording of the music must be licensed. In this case, the appropriate license would be a Master Use License.

Publisher — A Music Publisher owns the publishing rights to music. These rights usually entitle the Publisher to decide how a piece of music can be distributed or used in various forms, including use as a Source cue in a film or television project. A publisher can be a company or an individual, and collects Publisher Royalties from the performing rights organizations based on public performances of the music (see *Performing Rights Royalties*). Publishers may also license the music to others for use in film and television productions. This type of license is called a Synchronization License. The music publisher for each cue in a film or television project is indicated on the Cue Sheet.

Punches (see *Streamers*)

Reverb (or *Reverberation*) — An electronic effect that adds an *echo* to sound. Reverb is often used to simulate the effect of music or sound being played in a room, hall, or auditorium.

Royalties — Payments to the publisher(s) and composer(s) of a musical composition. Royalties can come from various sources, including royalties paid from the sales of CDs, royalties paid from broadcasts on metered services such as pay-per-view television, and performing rights royalties.

Sampler — An electronic device which plays back digital recordings of musical instruments and other sounds. Samplers are often used as a substitute for live musicians in lower budget productions. Often confused with Synthesizers, which create electronic sounds (see *Synthesizer*).

Score Supervisor — A person who assists the composer at recording sessions by watching the printed score and listening to the performances of the musicians to aid the composer. The Score Supervisor often communicates with the composer or orchestra conductor through a private headphone mix that only the composer/conductor can hear. The composer/conductor then makes comments to the musicians as he/she deems necessary. The Score Supervisor may occasionally make comments to the Scoring Engineer about the volume levels of different instruments and other technical aspects of the recording process.

Scoring Engineer (or *Scoring Mixer*) — The person who records, mixes (adjusts levels, effects, and tone), and has overall responsibility for microphone placement and recording the musicians at a recording session. Also known as a Recording Engineer.

Scoring Stage — A recording studio with a room designed for orchestral recordings. Usually the room is large and equipped with a podium and other microphones and equipment necessary to record an orchestra.

Sequencer — A device or computer program used by a composer to record the parts to be played by musicians or to be electronically played on samplers or synthesizers. Sequencers can play back complex musical compositions at virtually any speed, allow quick changing of notes and instruments, and in some cases can print the music out as a score and parts.

Sidelining — A term used to describe musicians appearing on-screen in a film or television production. The musicians usually appear with their musical instruments, and may or may not actually play the instruments.

Signatory — A signatory is a business or individual who is authorized by the American Federation of Musicians to act as an employer of musicians. In certain A F of M contracts and agreements such as the Assumption Agreement, the signatory becomes legally responsible for possible future payments to the musicians.

SMPTE (or *Time Code*) — SMPTE stands for The Society of Motion Picture and Television Engineers, and usually refers to time code, for which this organization developed various standards.

The terms SMPTE and time code are often used interchangeably. SMPTE is recorded as an audio signal, and is also usually shown in a *window* on the screen for reference purposes. An example of a time code location might be **01:00:16:23**, which refers to a time code location of "One Hour, zero minutes, sixteen seconds, and twenty-three frames." SMPTE is used to refer to specific locations in a piece of video or audio product, and comes in several types including Drop Frame and Non-Drop Time Code.

Sound Designer — A Sound Designer creates sounds or sound effects (usually not musical pieces) for use in film and television projects. The Sound Designer will often work with the composer to ensure that the music composed for a project is compatible with (and does not interfere with) any special sounds or sound effects.

Spotting Session — The Spotting Session usually takes place after the filming and editing phases of a production have been completed. At the Spotting Session, the director and composer agree on what types of music will be used in a project and on where in the film (usually time code locations) specific musical cues will occur. The Music Editor documents these decisions and provides Spotting Notes to the composer and director for reference.

Streamer — A thin line which moves from left to right across an image of the film seen by the orchestra conductor at recording sessions. Streamers are used to provide the orchestra conductor with timing information as he/she conducts the musicians. At the end of a streamer, a *punch* — a large dot that flashes in the film image — is added to signify a *hit* or specific point in the film that the music may be synchronized with. When conducting *free-time* (without click in the musicians' or conductor's headphones), the conductor can synchronize the music to the film with the aid of streamers and punches.

Swimming — A term used to describe music or sound that has too much reverb or echo.

Synchronization Rights (or *Sync Rights*) — Refers to the privilege of using an existing piece of music, often a Source Cue, in timed relation with the picture in a film or television production. Synchronization rights are usually negotiated with the publisher of the music. A license to record or use music in sync with picture is called a Synchronization License. An example of a Synchronization License is shown in section III of this Guide.

Synthesizer — An electronic device which generates or creates a sound. Often confused with samplers, which play back a digital recording of an actual real-world sound, such as a violin being played or a drum being hit. Synthesizers were very popular in the 1970's and 1980's and were used to imitate and substitute for live instruments. With the advent of digital samplers, synthesizers are now used primarily for special effects and electronic sounds.

Temp Track (or *Temp Music*) — Music added to a film or television project before the actual music is composed. Temp music is often added before screening the film to test audiences and film production executives. Getting involved in the selection of temp music can be helpful to the composer in understanding the music needs of the director, however some composers prefer not to be involved in the temp music selection process.

Timing Notes (see *Breakdown Notes*)

Walla (or *wallah*) — Background group sounds, usually muttering voices, that add ambience to a scene.

MUSIC EDITOR TERMS AND ABBREVIATIONS

BG   background

CAM   camera

CU   close-up

CUT   immediate change (cut) from one shot to another

DIAL   dialogue

DISS   dissolve — simultaneous fade-in and fade-out of consecutive shots

DUBBING   final mix of the film that combines music, dialog and sound-effects into a single sound track

DUBBING SHEET   a report usually created by the Music Editor which contains the final specifications of the music used in a film or television production. The dubbing sheet includes the title, track location, and a visual representation of the cues in show order with their SMPTE time code starts and stops clearly identified (see section II of this Guide for an example).

EL   end of line of dialogue

EOR   end of reel

EXT   exterior

FI   fade-in from black

FF   freeze frame — one frame is multiple-printed to appear as a still picture

FO   fade-out to black

FX   effects — sound effects

HIT

a time code location or action that the music should emphasize or acknowledge

INT

interior

MATTE SHOT

shots in which portions of frame show different images using matte techniques

LS

long shot, full shot; a shot from a significant distance away

MS or MED

medium shot

MOS

without sound

MX

music

NARR

narration

OS

off-stage

PAN

panorama shot — camera rotates, revealing sweep of scene

PIX

picture

POV

from the point of view of the named actor

PRELAP

when music starts just shortly before a scene, right at the tail end of the previous scene

REACTION SHOT

frame shows a secondary figure reacting to a previous shot

SIDE

side shot

SOURCE MUSIC

music that appears to come from the scene; music the actors hear

STREAMER

vertical line that moves across the screen from left to right. This gives the composer a visual reference of an upcoming *hit* or downbeat.

TEMP TRACK

temporary music that a film editor or Music Editor will add to a film at an early stage. Filmmakers use this to convey their musical wishes to a composer and to screen the unfinished film to studio executives and test audiences.

TESLA BOX   a device used by Music Editors to create digital clicks and stream-
                         ers

UNDERSCORE   supporting music which the audience hears but the actors don't

VO   voice-over — a voice that does not lip-sync with a subject in the
                         frame

WS   wide shot

XCU or ECU   extreme close-up

XLS or ELS   extreme long shot

ZOOM IN   optical effect of coming closer to subject

ZOOM OUT   optical effect of subject becoming farther away

AN INTRODUCTION TO ASCAP, BMI, AND SESAC

ASCAP, BMI, and SESAC are performing rights organizations in the United States. Their main function is to collect performing rights royalties from those who commercially use the music of their member writers and publishers. They distribute royalties to their members after administration costs are deducted.

Performing rights organizations license *public performances* of their members' music in the United States for non-dramatic rights, which generally includes use on domestic television, cable TV, pay-cable networks (such as HBO and Showtime) and use in commercial facilities such as nightclubs, restaurants, and music-on-hold services.

Dramatic Rights, which are not within the realm of the performing rights organizations, are performances such as Broadway and off-Broadway plays and ballets. Audio books sold for retail are not covered by the performing rights organizations unless they are broadcast on television or otherwise used in the situations described above.

In the United States, performances of music on television are covered while performances of music in movie theaters are not. In almost every other country, performances of music in movie theaters are covered by the local performing rights organization which has a reciprocal agreement with the U.S. performing rights organizations.

What do ASCAP, BMI, and SESAC mean to the film and television composer?

1.   Each music performance when a show or film is broadcast on television has the potential to generate performing rights royalties for the writer(s) and publisher(s) of the music. Live performances can also generate royalties.

2.   If a performance is logged (i.e. identified by ASCAP/BMI/SESAC as having been broadcast), a royalty will be paid based on the number of times the film or show is broadcast and other factors such as the length and type of music performed. There are very specific *weighting formulas* that are used to calculate the royalty payments for each performance of a composition. In some cases the historical popularity of a composition will increase the current royalties paid for performances of the composition. You should consult the performing rights organizations for specific rules and formulas that determine the calculation of royalties.

3.   Equal royalties are paid to the writer(s) and publisher(s) of the music, and are paid on

a quarterly basis. In order to collect publishing royalties, the composer or filmmaker must have a registered publishing company with ASCAP/BMI/SESAC.

What's the typical royalty situation for film and television projects today?

1.   With very few exceptions, composers insist on keeping their writer's royalties. Only in special circumstances such as when the composer is an employee of a larger organization (such as a staff composer for a company) is it customary for the composer to give up writer's royalties. The subject of whether ghostwriters, sub-composers, and others employed by some composers have a claim to writer's royalties is a frequently discussed topic. Anyone approached to do ghostwriting should always confirm what, if any, royalties will be paid.

2.   Today it is a common and accepted business practice that the filmmaker or television production company retain publishing rights to original music created for a film or television production. In this situation, the publisher's performing rights royalties would be paid to a publishing company owned by the film production company. The only requirement here is that the production company must set up a publishing company with ASCAP, BMI, or SESAC depending on the affiliation of the composer(s). Composers that retain the publishing on music they write will usually set up their own publishing company with the performing rights organization with whom they are affiliated.

3.   It's important to note that film and television production companies do not pay royalties of any kind to the performing rights organizations. All performing rights royalties distributed by these organizations are paid from usage fees collected from the end users of the music (such as television stations, restaurants, and end users in foreign countries).

Address and contact information for ASCAP, BMI, and SESAC can be found in the **Organizations** *section of this Guide. You can also look on each organization's internet web site for more information — the internet addresses are listed in the* **Internet Resources** *section of this Guide.*

MUSIC CLEARANCE FOR SONGS AND SOURCE MUSIC

While music clearance is usually the job of the Music Supervisor of a film or television production, composers and songwriters may occasionally be called upon to do some of the tasks of a Music Supervisor. This happens more frequently in low budget films with limited music budgets.

Music clearing is the process of negotiating and obtaining permission from a publisher to use one or more songs or source music cues in a film or television production, and negotiating a fee for that use. The end result is a synchronization license, in which all the terms for usage of the music are clearly stated.

If you wish to use an existing sound recording of the music in a film or television project, an additional license called a Master Use License from the owner of the sound recording is usually required. Examples of Synchronization and Master Use Licenses are included in section three of this Guide.

It is wise to start as early as possible with the licensing process, because many times music is published by more than one publisher and the process of negotiating with each publishing company can be quite time consuming.

Once you've identified the music you want to use, the first thing you'll need to do is identify the publisher(s) of the music. The best way to get publishing information is to call the offices of ASCAP, BMI, or SESAC, or use their online internet title search sites. Complete information for these organizations is listed in the **Organizations** section of this Guide. Be sure to have the names of the authors and the title, since many songs can have the same title. ASCAP, BMI and SESAC usually refer to the author(s) of music as *writers*.

Once you've obtained the publisher information, call the publisher(s) to determine what information they will need to give you a quote. Usually, publishers will require a written request letter stating all the terms of your proposed usage of the music. A typical quote request letter contains the following information:

- Title
- Author(s)
- Duration of the song (if unsure, decide on a maximum length the usage could be and state "up to but not more than...")
- Territory, for example, the world, the U.S., film festivals, the universe, etc.
- Proposed Advertising and marketing uses such as trailers and television/radio commercials

- Description of the scene where the music will be used (sometimes publishers will request script pages or rough video footage). Also included here would be whether you wish to use an existing sound recording or intend to re-record the song.
- Length of the license, usually in years or in perpetuity

You can find examples of quote letters in section three of this Guide.

After receiving a quote it is important to send a letter confirming all the terms of the license. The publisher or record company will then issue a license when the fee has been paid. At this point you may want to request that the publisher or record company supply you with exact information for the end title screen credits.

Other tips

Let the publisher know if a film will only be shown at festivals or is a student work. These types of projects have special rates that are often much lower than rates for commercial projects intended for theatrical, pay-TV, or other commercial distribution. Many filmmakers purchase *festival licenses* for music used in independently produced films in order to show the films at festivals and shows. When a distribution deal is made for the film, the distributor is usually responsible for re-negotiating final licenses for commercial usage of the music.

When contacting publishers, ask what percentage of the publishing rights for the music they own. You want to make sure 100% of the publishing is accounted for. Also, world publishing rights of some music is divided — one publisher may own the domestic publishing rights, while another may own the foreign rights.

If the music was recorded using union musicians, fees may have to be paid to the original musicians who recorded the music. Contact the American Federation of Musicians (see contact information in the **Organizations** section of this Guide) for more information.

A good source of information for music clearing and licensing is *MUSIC, MONEY, AND SUCCESS* by Jeffrey and Todd Brabec (Schirmer Books). It goes into detail about the types of licenses that exist and typical fees paid for music used in films, television, and commercials. We recommend this book highly.

CURRENT RATES

We've included some typical rates for various jobs associated with composing and recording film and television music. These rates are based on the current environment in Los Angeles, California in 1998. Many factors may influence the actual rates for your community, including:

- The business climate of your city and state
- Availability of professional musicians and other support personnel
- The type of project you are working on
- Your history or track record with musicians and other people who have worked with you in the past
- The availability of non-union musicians vs. union musicians
- The skill level and experience of the musicians and support personnel
- The difficulty of the music and amount of preparation needed by the musicians

COMPOSERS

The fees composers are paid for film and television productions vary widely, and are dependent on many factors, including whether the project is a *package* deal, union considerations, and most of all the market value of the composer. We've included some fee ranges that are current as of the printing of this Guide (1998, Los Angeles). As rates vary from community to community, you should investigate what the current rates are where you are planning to work.

Feature Film   The absolute low end is a $5,000 package with the composer usually keeping the publishing rights on all music. Most low budget films offer $10,000 - $75,000 package deals. Medium budget films range from $50,000 creative fee (not including musicians and recording costs) to $200,000 package deals. High end film composers (top 20 - 30 or so) make anywhere from $150,000 - $750,000 and more in creative fees for top feature films.

Television   Most television scoring today is done on a package deal basis. Half hour series television can pay from $2,000 - $8,000 per episode on a package basis. One hour comedy and dramatic series television can pay from $4,000 - $18,000 per episode on a package basis. For shows that utilize a full orchestra, composers are usually paid a creative fee of $5,000 - $15,000 per show and the production company pays for the cost of musicians and recording.

Television movies are usually done on a package basis, and pay from $10,000 - $30,000 per movie. Occasionally a television movie will have a higher music budget in the $50,000 - $100,000 range including musicians and recording costs.

It is important to note that these fees usually assume that the production company keeps publishing rights for the music. These fees do not include any performing rights royalties, which in film and television can be substantial. When you are determining what fee to charge for a project, don't forget to factor in the following items:

- All out-of-pocket costs, including musicians, engineer, studio expenses
- A contingency for overbudget costs
- Time necessary for changes and revisions
- Facilities and time necessary to prepare demos of cues on videotape
- Music editing and music preparation costs
- Future performing rights royalty income

MUSICIANS

The cost of musicians will often be the largest portion of your direct expenses in a project. Usually the only rule that can be used to estimate the cost of a musician is that more experienced musicians (and those who play a greater number of instruments) will expect to be paid higher rates for their services. Beyond that, it's all negotiation. Always consult with a qualified contractor or the A F of M for specific union rates if you are doing a project under a union contract. Union rates change frequently and are far too complicated to discuss in detail in this book.

We've broken the current rates down by types of projects you may encounter:

Scenario 1: Demo session — three hours to create demo recordings that will not be used as a final product

> **Non-Union:** $25 - $50/hour. Cartage additional for harp, keyboards, or any large percussion instruments ($50 is typical)

> **Union:** $25 - $35/hour plus benefits. Leader receives 150% of standard rate, 1 hour minimum call. *Rates outside of Los Angeles in different union locals may be different.*

Notes: Using live musicians on your demo recordings can be a great idea, time and finances permitting. Expect to pay higher rates for string players. Since rates are very low for this type of work, creating a musician-friendly environment at your recording sessions can go a long way towards building valuable relationships with musicians.

Scenario 2: Non-Union Film or Television project

Rates: Typical musician rates are $50 - $100/hour depending on the experience of the player. Expect to pay rates in the higher part of this range for string players. Cartage is additional for large percussion instruments and other large setups (guitar rig, keyboard rig, harp). Cartage fees are negotiable and can range from $50 to $250 per day.

Notes: The new Low Budget Film Agreement that the Musicians Union provides has made a significant portion of previously non-union work workable under union contracts. In some cases, however, the film-maker is unwilling to sign an Assumption Agreement which is still required under the Low Budget Film Agreement. Other situations, such as using a few live musicians overdubbed on top of samplers, are often recorded non-union on low budget films.

Scenario 3: Low Budget Union Film Project

Rates: If the project falls under the Low Budget Film Agreement (total budget of the film is less than ten million dollars), special rates of approx. $45 - $50/hour plus benefits for a minimum three hour session.

Notes: Consult with the A F of M to see if your project qualifies under this special agreement. Note that the filmmaker will be required to disclose budget details of the film to the union. You will probably want to use a contractor to calculate all union wage scales and complete the appropriate paperwork.

Scenario 4: Union Film Project

Rates: $75 - $85/hour plus benefits and overtime, plus additional fees (such as additional pay for leader and contractor, limits on number of minutes of music recorded per hour, and additional pay for doubling).

Notes: Due to the complexity of union wage rules, it is generally advisable to use a contractor whenever you do a union recording job. The contractor will complete all paperwork and calculate the appropriate union wage scales for the recording sessions and complete the appropriate forms and documentation.

A variety of other union rates exist for different types of projects, with special rates for businesses such as PBS (The Public Broadcasting System). It is a good idea to stay abreast of all the current union rates so you'll be ready to quote projects that will be done under a union recording contract. A handy reference of all the current union recording rates is available in the RMA (Recording Musicians Association) handbook. See the **Organizations** listing later in this section for information on how to contact the RMA. Currently it is not necessary to become a member of the RMA to purchase a directory.

One final note about union vs. non-union recordings for film and television projects — it is always a good idea to determine if the non-music members of the production are working under a union contract for the production. In rare instances, other unions have been known to force the composer to pay union wages for musicians, even retroactively to the beginning of a television series. One composer we know of found himself in this situation, and since he/she did the show under a *package* deal, was responsible for all of the retroactive pay himself. By being aware of all of the union aspects of a project, you can avoid this type of problem.

MUSIC EDITORS

Music Editors are usually members of the IATSE union, and are often asked to perform a number of different services, including:

- Attend Spotting Sessions
- Prepare Spotting and Breakdown notes
- Prepare temp music tracks
- Attend music recording sessions and track the progress of each cue
- Assist the composer in making changes to cues at the recording sessions

- Communicate with the filmmaker in discussions of timings and cue beginning/ending issues
- Do digital editing of finished music cues for various reasons
- Work at the prelay session to insert music at the correct locations
- Work at the film mixing sessions to answer any questions about music placement and timings
- Prepare performing rights cue sheets
- Prepare dubbing sheets
- Prepare final delivery cue sheets

Prices for Music Editors are negotiable depending on which services you ask them to perform. On a per-project basis, rates can range from a one-time fee of $750 - $1,500 for spotting and breakdown notes only, to $1,500 - $3,000/week for full-service music editing. There may be additional rental charges if any digital editing equipment such as Pro Tools is required.

Some Music Editors will work in a non-union situation, so consult with any Music Editors you are considering for a non-union project to see if they are willing to work in a non-union situation if necessary. It would generally not be advisable to hire musicians in a non-union situation and hire the Music Editor under a union contract.

CONTRACTORS

The primary functions of a contractor are:

1. Hiring of musicians as directed by the composer for recording sessions
2. Providing any A F of M rate and scale information to the composer and filmmaker as necessary
3. Completion of all necessary A F of M paperwork and contracts
4. Working with the payroll company (if applicable) to ensure that the musician payroll is properly prepared and delivered
5. Working with composer and filmmaker to contract for recording studio space
6. Attending recording sessions

One of the best reasons to use a contractor is that contractors are usually experts at putting together ensembles of musicians that work well together. It is the contractor's responsibility to be extremely familiar with the strengths and weaknesses of musicians in the community, and to know which musicians work well together and which might not.

A contractor must be very familiar with the A F of M rates and regulations, and can serve as a valuable source of information when calculating union rates for budgeting and planning purposes. The contractor can also assist in negotiating rates with musicians where appropriate (often the fees for doubles and cartage are negotiable).

Union rates: Generally a contractor is paid 150% of a single musician's scale wages for each recording session. If the contractor is also playing in the orchestra, the total pay for the contractor would be 200% of scale. Consult union regulations for more information.

Non-Union: Some contractors will work in a non-union situation. Rates are approximately the same as for union work, but can be negotiable. Note that for especially small groups (under 10 players) a contractor may not be a playing member of the group so a separate fee negotiation is advisable. Hourly rates for contracting services are very rare — generally rates are based on the musicians' pay for the recording sessions.

ORCHESTRATORS

In today's MIDI oriented world, the job of orchestrating has become very hard to define in many cases. Since the work of orchestrating can involve everything from MIDI file interpretation (including making changes when necessary because of errors in instrument range and other problems) to reading and working from sketches which may be detailed or not, rates often fall in a wide range.

The most common rate structure for orchestrating is the *page rate*, which basically charges per page (usually 4 bars) of music. The basic page rate can range anywhere from $25 - $75 per page depending on the skill of the orchestrator and the actual work involved.

Additional fees may be charged if the orchestrator is asked to work from MIDI files or if additional *fix-up* work is necessary. Types of fix-up work include identifying music that is out of an instrument's playable range, and fixing note value problems when a computer MIDI file has notes indicated at unrealistic or unreadable durations.

Union orchestration rates for film and television projects range from approx. $22 - $50/page plus benefits.

The most important part of negotiating with an orchestrator is to define exactly what work you are contracting the orchestrator to do. Provide the orchestrator with an example of the format you will be giving him/her the music in, whether it be on paper or diskette. By discussing all the details at the beginning of a project, you can avoid potential problems or disagreements later.

COPYISTS (MUSIC PREPARATION)

Copyists also work on a *page rate* fee structure and charge per page of finished part or score that is created. Most copyists are members of the American Federation of Musicians (A F of M).

Generally a page in copyist terms is from 6 to 10 staves with 4 bars of music on each staff. Most copyists charge union rates for union and non-union jobs. Typical rates are anywhere from $5 - $15 per page, with additional fees for duplicate parts, transpositions, and score preparation.

Some copyists will quote a flat rate per page of part preparation including all transpositions. Flat rates for copyists can range from $7 - $10 per page.

The A F of M has a complex schedule of copying rates and additional fees. If you hire a copyist under a union contract, make sure you get detailed information in advance on how you will be charged. It is inadvisable to hire musicians under a non-union situation and a copyist under a union contract for the same project, as the A F of M is the union for both groups.

You should discuss with your copyist exactly what services you require, and may want to ask that the copyist attend the recording sessions in case parts need to be changed.

Rates tend to be the same for computer generated parts and handwritten parts. Musicians tend to prefer computer generated parts when sight-reading more difficult music. The main advantage to computer generated parts is that they can be quickly changed and re-printed at the recording session if necessary.

If you are doing your own music preparation, you may be interested to know that for many of our projects, preparing computer generated parts complete with dynamic markings, phrasing, and expressions usually takes twice as long as preparing handwritten parts.

ENGINEERS

Recording engineers are almost always paid on an hourly basis. Some recording engineers belong to a union, but many do not. Most recording engineers are willing to work on non-union recording sessions, however.

Some recording engineers are willing to work on demo projects for a reduced rate. Typical rates for demo projects are $30 - $60/hour.

Rates for non-demo film and television projects vary widely, and are typically in the range of $40 - $80/hour. Some extremely popular high-end engineers command rates of $75 - 150/hour and more, but this type of rate is the exception rather than the rule. High-end engineers may also work on a per-day rate of $1,200 - 1,500 per day.

ASSISTANTS

Working as a composer's assistant usually involves doing a wide range of work. While many assistant positions involve clerical and maintenance work (everything from doing the bookkeeping to washing the composer's car), some positions offer more attractive work such as working with the composer on composing and orchestrating functions.

Assistants are either hired on an *as needed* basis or may work regular hours as either a part-time or full-time employee. Typical hourly pay rates for composer's assistants are $10 - $15/hour for routine work. For work that requires a higher degree of skill, such as with composing, orchestrating, or engineering, composer assistant rates can range from $15 - $30/hour.

One important aspect of hiring an assistant is to determine the assistant's legal tax status. If the assistant is being hired to do work in a situation where he/she should be treated as an employee (for tax purposes), using an employee leasing firm or payroll service can minimize the amount of bookkeeping necessary to properly account for the assistant as an employee.

If you hire an assistant as an independent contractor and do not deduct taxes and withholding, make sure your relationship with the assistant qualifies for this tax treatment with the IRS. If your assistant does not qualify for independent contractor treatment and is deemed an employee by the IRS (which can occur long after the assistant has left your employ), you may be liable for severe retroactive tax penalties. Consult your accountant or tax attorney for specific information on this subject.

FIFTY PLACES AND USES FOR ORIGINAL MUSIC

Sometimes it can be helpful to remember that there is a huge and growing market for original music. We've included some ideas here that may be beneficial to you as you consider who you want to market your music to...

1. Feature Films
2. Student Films
3. Television Series
4. Television Pilots
5. Infomercials
6. Local Cable or Cable Access Shows
7. Awards Shows and Ceremonies
8. Video/Television Music Concerts
9. Corporate Promotional Videos
10. How-To Videos for Consumers
11. Instructional and Motivational Videos for Businesses
12. Exercise and Fitness Videos
13. Airlines in-flight Entertainment channels
14. Background and Foreground music suppliers such as Muzak
15. Television Commercials
16. Radio Commercials and Background Music
17. Music On-Hold Services
18. Theme Parks — background/ambience music
19. Special Rides and Attractions at fairs and theme parks
20. Internet Web Pages and Web Sites that broadcast content
21. Automated Kiosks and Retail Displays
22. CD-ROMs for computer software companies
23. Computer Games
24. Instructional CD-ROMs
25. Cartridge-type/propriety Game Devices (such as Nintendo)
26. Recording Artist (instrumental or vocal)
27. Interactive CD-ROM Films
28. Background Music for 1-900 pay telephone services
29. Radio Show Parody and Novelty/Comedy Acts
30. Musical Theater Productions
31. Audition Tapes for Performers
32. Vocalists who need Demo Tapes
33. Conferences and Expos

34. Lyricists looking for music for their lyrics
35. Live Shows, such as theme park performing groups
36. Community-sponsored productions, such as summer theaters and plays
37. Big Bands, Dance Bands, Jazz Bands, and Rock/Pop Bands
38. Documentaries and educational films
39. Books on Tape (also known as Audio Books)
40. Meetings and Corporate Events
41. Toys that have integrated music playback capabilities
42. Local Television Station Broadcasts, such as news and community shows
43. Local Radio Broadcasts, such as theme packages, traffic report music, etc.
44. Corporate and Film Company Logo Music
45. Circuses and Fairs
46. Specialty Performers, such as children's entertainers
47. Symphony Orchestras and Concert Music
48. Arcade Games and Machines
49. Demo Sequences for synthesizers and samplers
50. Game Shows

SCHOOLS THAT OFFER PROGRAMS IN MUSIC FOR FILM AND TELEVISION

These colleges offer various programs and degrees in the study of film and television music. While many schools are now beginning to offer classes and various seminars in the area of film and television music, the schools listed below have established programs that offer a comprehensive study program for those wishing to pursue an academic education in film and television music.

Berklee College of Music
Film Scoring Department
1140 Boylston Street
Boston, MA 02215
617-266-1400

UCLA Extension
Film Scoring Program
10995 Le Conte Avenue
Room 437
P.O. Box 24901
Los Angeles, CA 90099
310-206-4906

USC School of Music
Office of Admissions
University Park Campus
Los Angeles, CA 90089
213-740-8986

FILM AND TELEVISION MUSIC AGENTS

There are a relatively few number of agents that specialize in film and television composers. Remember that usually agents choose only to work with those composers who already have an established track record and have achieved significant name recognition in the industry. If you have a limited track record and are offered (or hired for) a significant project, you might want to consider approaching a film and television agent to do a *one-off* (one-time) deal. Some agents are amenable to this type of deal as it gives both of you the opportunity work together in a non-exclusive environment.

One of the best ways to approach an agent is to ask in the nicest way possible for some career advice. Although some agents will only speak with clients, it can't hurt to try and approach them if you are appreciative for any time they may spend with you.

Air Edel
11620 Wilshire Boulevard
Suite 230
Los Angeles, CA 90025
310-914-5000

The Artists Group
10100 Santa Monica Boulevard
Suite 2490
Los Angeles, CA 90067
310-552-1100

Creative Artists Agency
9830 Wilshire Boulevard
Beverly Hills, CA 90212
310-288-4545

Carol Faith Agency
280 South Beverly Drive
Suite 411
Beverly Hills, CA 90212
310-274-0776

Film Music Associates
6525 Sunset Boulevard
Third Floor
Hollywood, CA 90028
213-463-1070

Gorfaine/Schwartz
13245 Riverside Drive
Suite 450
Sherman Oaks, CA 91423
818-461-9600

Seth Kaplan Entertainment
106 South Orange Drive
Los Angeles, CA 90036
213-525-3477

Jeff H. Kaufman, A Talent Agency
12007 Laurel Terrace Drive
Studio City, CA 91604
818-506-6013

Ken Kushnick Management
1840 Fairburn Avenue
Suite 303
Los Angeles, CA 90025
310-470-5909

The Kohner Agency
9300 Wilshire Boulevard
Suite 555
Beverly Hills, CA 90212
310-550-1060

The Kordek Agency
211 West Alameda Avenue
Burbank, CA 91502
818-526-1626

Kraft-Benjamin Agency
345 North Maple Drive
Suite 385
Beverly Hills, CA 90210
310-247-0123

Robert Light Agency
6404 Wilshire Boulevard
Suite 900
Los Angeles, CA 90048
213-651-1777

Ocean Park Music Group
1861 South Bundy Drive
Suite 109
Los Angeles, CA 90025
310-315-5266

Derek Power Company
11450 Albata Street
Los Angeles, CA 90049
310-472-4647

Cathy Schleussner
Soundtrack Music Assoc.
8938 Keith Avenue
West Hollywood, CA 90069
310-724-5600

The Shukat Company Ltd.
340 West 55th Street
Suite 1A
New York, NY 10019
212-582-7614

SMC Artists
4400 Coldwater Canyon
Suite 127
Studio City, CA 91604
818-505-9600

Twin Towers Management
8833 Sunset Boulevard
Penthouse West
Los Angeles, CA 90069
310-659-9644

Vangelos Management
16030 Ventura Boulevard
Suite 235
Encino, CA 91436
818-380-1919

Zomba Screen Music
9000 Sunset Boulevard
Suite 300
West Hollywood, CA 90069
310-247-4300

FILM AND TELEVISION MUSIC ATTORNEYS

We've listed some Los Angeles area attorneys who work in the area of film and television music. It is important to choose an attorney carefully, as many of your deals and contracts will require review by an experienced attorney. You may also want to ask about additional services, such as contract negotiation and music publishing administration.

The Winogradsky Company
Steve Winogradsky
11240 Magnolia Boulevard
Suite 104
North Hollywood, CA 91601
818-761-6906

**Bloom, Hergott, Cook,
Diemer and Klein**
Candice Hanson
150 South Rodeo Drive
Third Floor
Beverly Hills, CA 90212
310-859-6828

David A. Braun
1901 Avenue of the Stars
Suite 1501
Los Angeles, CA 90067
310-551-0715

Codikow, Carroll and Guido
9113 Sunset Boulevard
Los Angeles, CA 90069
310-271-0241

Garvin, Davis and Benjamin
9200 Sunset Boulevard
Penthouse 25
Los Angeles, CA 90069
310-278-7300

Gang, Tyre, Ramer and Brown
Don Passman
132 South Rodeo Drive
Beverly Hills, CA 90212
310-777-4800

Jeff Graubart
2029 Century Park East
Suite 2700
Los Angeles, CA 90067
310-788-2650

**Hansen, Jacobsen,
Teller and Hoberman**
Fred Goldring or Ken Hertz
450 North Roxbury Drive
8th Floor
Beverly Hills, CA 90210
310-271-8777

Kulik, Gottesman and Mouton
Megan O'Brien
1880 Century Park East
Suite 1150
Los Angeles, CA 90067
310-557-9200

Manatt, Phelps and Phillips
Lee Phillips
11355 West Olympic Boulevard
Los Angeles, CA 90064
310-312-4000

Mitchell, Silbenberg and Knupp
Gene Salomon and Danna Cook
11377 W. Olympic Boulevard
Los Angeles, CA 90064
310-312-3220

Gary Wishik
9107 Wilshire Boulevard
Suite 300
Beverly Hills, CA 90210
310-278-3092

ORGANIZATIONS

These organizations may be of interest to film and television composers.

American Society of Music Arrangers and Composers (ASMAC)
P.O. Box 17840
Encino, CA 91416
818-994-4661

American Federation of Musicians (New York)
1501 Broadway, Suite 600
New York, NY 10036
212-869-1330

Amercian Federation of Musicians (West Coast Office)
1777 North Vine Street
Suite 500
Hollywood, CA 90028
213-461-3441

ASCAP (Los Angeles)
7920 Sunset Boulevard
Suite 300
Los Angeles, CA 90046
213-883-1000

ASCAP (New York)
1 Lincoln Plaza
New York, NY 10023
212-621-6000

BMI (New York)
320 West 57th Street
New York, NY 10019
212-586-2000

BMI (Los Angeles)
8730 Sunset Boulevard
Third Floor
Los Angeles, CA 90069
310-659-9109

Film Music Network
1146 N. Central Ave. #103
Glendale, CA 91202
818-771-7778

The Harry Fox Agency, Inc.
711 3rd Avenue, 8th Floor
New York, NY 10017
212-370-5330

Musicians Union, Local 47, A.F. of M.
817 North Vine Street
Hollywood, CA 90038
213-462-2161

Nashville Songwriters Association, International
15 Music Square West
Nashville, TN 37203
615-256-3354

National Academy of Recording Arts & Sciences (NARAS)
3402 Pico Boulevard
Santa Monica, CA 90405
310-392-3777

National Academy of Songwriters
6255 Sunset Boulevard
Suite 1023
Hollywood, CA 90028
213-463-7178

Recording Musicians Association (RMA)
817 Vine Street, Suite 209
Hollywood, CA 90038
213-462-4762

SESAC (Nashville)
55 Music Square East
Nashville, TN 37203
615-320-0055

SESAC (New York)
421 W. 54th Street
New York, NY 10019
212-586-3450

The Society of Composers and Lyricists
400 South Beverly Drive
Suite 214
Beverly Hills, CA 90212
310-281-2812

Songwriters Guild of America (Los Angeles)
6430 Sunset Boulevard
Hollywood, CA 90028
213-462-1108

Songwriters Guild of America (Nashville)
1222 16th Avenue South, Suite 25
Nashville, TN 37212
615-329-1782

U.S. Copyright Office
Register of Copyrights
Library of Congress
Washington, D.C. 20559
202-707-3000

Volunteer Lawyers for the Arts
HEADQUARTERS
1 East 53rd Street
6th Floor
New York, NY 10022
212-319-2787

BOOKS

We've listed some of our favorite books that discuss film and television music and related areas.

BUSINESS ISSUES

Music, Money, and Success
Jeffrey Brabec and Todd Brabec
Schirmer Books
1633 Broadway
New York, NY 10019

This book is rapidly becoming the #1 source reference on the business of the music business. Excellent info on contracts, performing rights organizations, rates, and music publishing.

Get It In Writing
Brian McPherson
Hal Leonard Corporation
7777 W. Bluemound Road
Milwaukee, WI 53213

Music Publishing: A Songwriter's Guide - 2nd Edition
Randy Poe
Writer's Digest Books
1507 Dana Avenue
Cincinnati, Ohio 45207

Good information for songwriters

This Business of Music
Sidney Shemel and M. William Krasilovsky
Billboard Publications, Inc.
1515 Broadway
New York, NY 10036

One of the standards — has comprehensive music business information.

All You Need to Know About the Music Business
Donald S. Passman
Simon & Schuster
1230 Avenue of the Americas
New York, New York 10020

Great overview of the business

More About This Business of Music
Sidney Shemel and M. William Krasilovsky
Billboard Publications, Inc.
1515 Broadway
New York, NY 10036

MARKETING AND NETWORKING

Networking in the Music Business
Dan Kimpel
Writer's Digest Books
1507 Dana Avenue
Cincinnati, Ohio 45207

A very informative book about the music industry and how to market yourself

Musician's Guide to the Internet
Gary Hustwit
Hal Leonard Corporation
7777 W. Bluemound Road
Milwaukee, WI 53213

101 Ways to Promote Yourself
Avon Books (1997)
1350 Avenue of the Americas
New York, New York 10019

A great book with lots of good ideas about self promotion and marketing.

GUIDES AND DIRECTORIES

Hollywood Creative Directory
3000 West Olympic Boulevard
Santa Monica, California 90404
310-315-4815, 800-815-0503 (outside CA.)

This film and television industry bible lists producers, studio and network executives, production companies, studios and networks.

Film Composers Guide
Vincent J. Francillon and Steven C. Smith
Lone Eagle Publishing Company
2337 Roscomare Road, Suite 9
Los Angeles, CA 90077
310-471-8066

Directors Guild of America Directory
Directors Guild of America
7920 Sunset Boulevard
Los Angeles, CA 90046
310-289-2000

A directory of members, including contact info (often an agent or manager). If you are looking for a particular director, this is a great place to start.

Film Directors: A Complete Guide
Michael Singer
Lone Eagle Publishing Company
2337 Roscomare Road, Suite 9
Los Angeles, CA 90077
310-471-8066

Excellent resource for locating film directors.

Film/TV Music Guide
SRS Publishing
7510 Sunset Boulevard
Suite 1041
Los Angeles, CA 90046
800-377-7411

Includes a variety of different listings including music supervisors, publicists, publishers, and film/television composer agents.

Hollywood New Media Directory
Hollywood Creative Directory
3000 West Olympic Boulevard, Suite 2525
Santa Monica, California 90404
310-315-4815, 800-815-0503 (outside CA.)

A comprehensive resource about companies involved in new media including games, online services, internet content providers, and more.

IDA Membership Directory and Survival Guide
International Documentary Association
1551 South Robertson Boulevard
Los Angeles, CA 90035
310-284-8422

This membership directory lists members' name, phone, address and credits.

Professional Musicians Local 47 Directory
817 North Vine Street
Hollywood, CA 90038
213-462-2161

The best (and sometimes only!) way to locate Los Angeles area musicians, especially those involved in legit (symphony) or film/television scoring work. Only available to members of the Union and Union signatories.

RMA Directory
Recording Musicians Association
817 Vine Street, Suite 209
Hollywood, CA 90038
213-462-4RMA

Directory of members, associations, composer representation, recording studios, rehearsal studios, scoring stages, TV studios, theaters and concert halls, music preparation services, messenger services, payroll, record companies, cartage, storage and rentals, music equipment sales and services, and support services. Includes a very useful section listing current Musicians Union recording rates and rules.

THE HISTORY OF FILM AND TELEVISION SCORING

Film Score: The Art & Craft of Movie Music
Tony Thomas
Riverwood Press
Burbank, CA

A wonderful book on the history of film music.

The Art of Film Music
George Burt
Northeastern University Press
Boston, Massachusetts

An extensive look at some of the master composers of film music of this century. Lots of good score examples.

TV's Biggest Hits
Jon Burlingame
Schirmer Books
1633 Broadway
New York, NY 10019

The definitive history of television scoring. Lots of interesting facts and historical insight.

American Film Music
William Darby and Jack Du Bois
McFarland & Company, Inc.
Box 611
Jefferson, NC 28640

Film Music: A Neglected Art
Roy M. Prendergast
W.W. Norton & Company
500 Fifth Avenue
New York, NY 10010

Settling the Score: Music and the Classical Hollywood Film
Kathryn Kalinak
The University of Wisconsin Press
114 North Murray Street
Madison, WI 53715

TECHNICAL BOOKS, *HOW-TO* BOOKS, AND BOOKS ON THE ART OF FILM SCORING

On the Track
Fred Karlin and Rayburn Wright
Schirmer Books
1633 Broadway
New York, NY 10019

This is the <u>bible</u> about the art of film scoring for many composers today. A complete, comprehensive reference book featuring lots of interviews and quotes, technical information, and case histories of different scoring projects.

Orchestration Handbook
Judy Green Music
1616 Cahuenga Blvd
Hollywood, CA 90028
213-466-2491

This handy book contains ranges for instruments, volume and tempo indications, mood indications, and a click track table. Invaluable reference to keep handy when writing for live instruments.

Listening to Movies
Fred Karlin
Schirmer Books
1633 Broadway
New York, NY 10019

A look at the world of film music from the film lover's perspective. Great cross-reference of film titles and composers.

Synchronization From Reel to Reel
A Complete Guide for The Synchronization of Audio, Film & Video
Jeffrey Rona
Hal Leonard Publishing Corporation
7777 West Bluemound Road
P.O. Box 13819
Milwaukee, WI 53213

A complete and easy-to-understand book that explains all about SMPTE, time code, and other synchronization issues.

Range and Transposition Guide to 250 Musical Instruments
Robert G. Bornstein
Judy Green Music
1634 Cahuenga Boulevard
Hollywood, CA 90028

Great resource for locating information on how to write for hard-to-find instruments

Harp Scoring
Stanley Chaloupka
c/o Sylvia Woods Harp Center
915 N. Glendale Avenue
Glendale, CA
818-956-1363

Ever wonder how to correctly write and notate a harp part? Here are the answers. Very handy for those learning to write for the harp.

Getting the Best Score for Your Film: A Filmmakers' Guide to Music Scoring

David Bell
Silman-James Press
7623 Sunset Boulevard
Hollywood, CA 90046

An excellent book written for film directors and others who hire composers for film and television projects.

The Professional Arranger Composer

Russell Garcia
Criterion Music Corporation
6124 Selma Avenue
Hollywood, CA 90028

A good reference book for writing and arranging for big bands.

Music in Film and Video Productions

Dan Carlin, Sr.
Butterworth-Heinemann
80 Montvale Avenue
Stoneham, MA 02180

Scoring for Films

Earle Hagen
Alfred Publishing Company, Inc.
16380 Roscoe Boulevard
Van Nuys, CA 91410

A great perspective on the business from one of the greats.

Sounds and Scores
Henry Mancini
Northridge Music, Inc.
c/o All Nations Music
8857 West Olympic Boulevard
Beverly Hills, CA 90211

The Technique of Orchestration
Kent Kennan and Donald Grantham
Prentice Hall
Englewood Cliffs, NJ 07632

This textbook emphasizes the fundamentals of orchestration. The authors discuss instruments individually, by section, and finally in a full orchestral context. Suitable for beginning orchestration courses, the book also contains more advanced material.

The Study of Orchestration
Samuel Adler
W.W. Norton & Co.
New York, NY
800-223-2584

A standard reference on orchestrating.

Music Arranging and Orchestration
John Cacavas
Belwin Mills
Miami, Florida 33014

A great book that discusses orchestrating and arranging from a film composer's point of view.

Orchestration
Cecil Forsyth
Dover Publications, Inc.
180 Varick Street
New York, NY 10014

Music Notation: A Manual of Modern Practice
Gardner Read
Taplinger Publishing Company, Inc.
New York, New York

A standard reference for music notation.

The Art of Music Copying
Clinton Roemer
Roerick Music Co.
4046 Davana Road
Sherman Oaks, CA 91423

How to Make Money Scoring Soundtracks
Jeffrey Fisher
Mix Books
6400 Hollis Street, Suite 12
Emeryville, CA 94608

MAGAZINES AND PERIODICALS

Film Music Magazine
1146 N. Central Ave. #103
Glendale, CA 91202
1-888-678-6158

Published by the Film Music Network, this monthly trade publication includes comprehensive coverage of industry news, feature articles on established and up-and-coming film music personalities, investigative reporting about subjects of concern to film and television music professionals, and a complete calendar of film and television music events.

The Hollywood Reporter (Film and Television Music Issues)
5055 Wilshire Boulevard
Los Angeles, CA 90036
213-525-2000

Besides being an excellent daily entertainment trade paper, twice a year The Hollywood Reporter publishes a Film & TV Music Special Issue (in January and August) which contains composer interviews, the year's hot composers, who's who in composing, executive listings and more. Film & TV updates are also published twice a year.

The Music Report
Attn: Adam Wolff
1120 S. Robertson Blvd
Third Floor
Los Angeles, CA 90035
310-276-9166

This weekly publication is available to established music publishing companies and lists film, television, and multimedia projects currently seeking songs and original music. One of the best resources for music and score placement. Also lists companies seeking star musical performers for live performances and shows.

Music Connection
4731 Laurel Canyon Boulevard
North Hollywood, CA 91707
818-755-0101

Bi-monthly west coast music trade magazine containing A&R Reports, signings and assignments, demo critiques, disk reviews, club reviews and more.

Drama-Logue
1456 North Gordon Street
Los Angeles, CA 90028
213-464-5079

LA's premier weekly casting newspaper. Contains ads for composers. This is a good place to find out about upcoming films.

Film Score Monthly
5455 Wilshire Boulevard
Suite 1500
Los Angeles, CA 90036
213-937-9890

Features good sources for out-of-print CDs, interviews with composers, and information on upcoming scores and albums. Also available online at www.filmscoremonthly.com.

Backstage West
P.O. Box 5017
Brentwood, TN 37024
800-458-7541

Weekly casting newspaper. Contains ads for composers. Also covers the musical theater business.

Daily Variety
P.O. Box 6400
Torrance, CA 90504
800-323-4345

Excellent daily trade paper for the film and television business.

Electronic Musician
6400 Hollis Street #12
Emeryville, CA 94608
800-843-4086

Contains good information on home and project studio equipment.

Filmmaker
5455 Wilshire Boulevard
Suite 1500
Los Angeles, CA 90036

Magazine of Independent films which has production updates, information on festivals, independent film news and more.

International Documentary
1551 South Robertson Boulevard
Suite 201
Los Angeles, CA 90035
310-284-8422

Monthly magazine of the International Documentary Film Association containing member news, events and screenings, festivals and competitions, and articles on current films.

Keyboard Magazine
GPI Publications
20085 Stevens Creek
Cupertino, CA 95014

Mix Magazine
6400 Hollis Street #12
Emeryville, CA 94608
800-843-4086

Roland Users Group — *The Loop* Magazine
7200 Dominion Circle
Los Angeles, CA 90040

If you use any Roland sampler equipment, make sure you subscribe to this valuable resource. Contains hard-to-find information for Roland sampler owners.

COMPUTER HARDWARE AND SOFTWARE

With the almost daily changes in computer and music technology, it is impossible to present a complete list of equipment or software that will remain current for any period of time. For this type of information, we recommend magazines such as *Keyboard* and *Electronic Musician*. Computer information for IBM-compatibles and Macintosh computers, the most common computers for music applications, is available in leading magazines.

We've chosen to describe some different types of hardware and software that you may want to consider using in your studio. Also, we've listed some unusual and unique items that may you may find useful.

COMPUTER HARDWARE

Most film and television composers use either the Macintosh or IBM-compatible (PC) computer systems. Our experience is that the majority of film and television composers we work with and know of use the Macintosh. We use Macintosh systems in our studios and offices.

It is important to point out, however, that recent advances in technology and software development for PC based systems have made them competitive with Macintosh systems in the areas of software availability and features.

The two main functions of computer systems in film and television composers' studios is for sequencing/notation and digital audio recording/processing.

COMPUTER SOFTWARE

These are the major types of computer software programs that are used in film and television music studios:

Sequencing

These programs allow for the recording and playback of music on MIDI equipment and with digital audio soundfiles. Your sequencer program will usually be the heart of your studio, and will be the software you use most frequently. Some issues that are important in sequencing software are:

- Speed and performance
- Ability to create legible printed music
- Ability to edit music in different ways, including via notation (notes printed on staff), notes by range, and by MIDI event.
- Digital audio recording and playback capabilities
- Compatibility with other software, such as notation and digital audio recording.

Notation

Notation software allows you to create professional looking printed music. Some notation programs can be very complex and difficult to use, but the majority of programs are reasonably easy to learn and use. While some people use the built-in notation capabilities of sequencer programs to print quick parts and scores, dedicated notation programs are generally the best way to produce professional, polished-looking parts and scores.

Digital Audio Recording/Playback

Digital Audio software allows you to record, edit, and play multiple tracks of digital audio. The editing capability of this software is especially important as digital editing of audio files is becoming an important tool in the creation of demos and alternate versions of cues. Many composers are now using computers with digital audio software as a replacement for multitrack tape recorders for recording and editing of music.

Music Editing Software

Music editing software is used to maintain information about cues and the timings for each cue. There are two main systems in use today for these tasks:

The Auricle, published by Auricle Control Systems, is a comprehensive system for creating and maintaining timing information for film music. You can use Auricle throughout the composing process to calculate timings and manage the overall structure of each cue. Auricle is used by almost every major film composer today, and is considered to be the standard tool for this type of work. Auricle runs on a separate IBM compatible computer, and can be used with both Macintosh and IBM systems since it communicates with your sequencing software via MIDI. The Auricle is available from:

Auricle Control Systems
3828 Woodcliff Road
Sherman Oaks, CA 91403
tel: 818-990-8442
fax: 818-990-0226
e-mail: auricle@ix.netcom.com

Cue, written by Rick Johnston, is a complete music editing program for the Macintosh computer. For more information on Cue, contact Rick at:

Rick Johnston
CUE
tel: 818-884-7664
e-mail: jlcrick@aol.com

OTHER HARDWARE/SOFTWARE

The **Click Kicker** is a device that accepts the speaker output of a computer or any other audio *tempo* type signal, and upon *hearing* the signal, generates a click sound that is suitable for headphones. The click sound generated by the Click Kicker resembles that of expensive digital metronomes used in high-end recording studios. By using the speaker of the computer to trigger the Click Kicker, you avoid having to use any MIDI channels or audio outputs on your synthesizers or samplers — very handy! Available from:

Brunswick Instrument, Inc.
Attn: Kelvin Palmer
6150 W. Mulford Street
Niles, IL 60714
tel: 847-965-9191
fax: 847-965-9193
e-mail: 71213.153@compuserve.com

There are a number of shareware and freeware utilities that are commonly available on the Internet for both IBM and Macintosh computers. Because web sites and resources on the internet change on a daily basis, we haven't attempted to list the many sources that exist for this software. A good place to start, however, is the file search areas on America Online and Compuserve. Among the most useful utilities we've found are:

Tap Tempo Calculators — these programs allow you to tap a tempo on the keyboard or mouse, and will calculate what tempo (usually in beats per minute) you are tapping. Some sequencer software programs include this feature, but we've found it easier to have a separate tap calculator program ready when needed.

Time Code Calculators — these handy utilities allow you to do addition and subtraction with time code. Very useful for tasks such as determining the exact (frame accurate) length of a cue, converting one type of time code to another, and calculating time code offsets and other adjustments.

Macintosh Filetype/Creator Utility — on the Macintosh computers each file has a file-type and creator, which are normally invisible to the user. Usually there is no need to modify these attributes, but when you create a Standard Midi File (SMF) on an IBM computer and load that disk into a Macintosh, your programs may not be able to see the file. These handy utility programs set a file's type to *Midi* (capitalized with a capital *M* only!) so your Macintosh programs can use the file.

Online Services — we recommend subscribing to at least one online service, such as America Online. Although internet technology is expanding and improving rapidly, sending files such as Standard MIDI Files over the Internet can be problematic. We've found that sending files in the form of attachments over an online service from one subscriber to another is much more dependable. We use America Online regularly during projects to receive MIDI files and breakdown notes from our Music Editor — it's much faster and cheaper than messenger or delivery services.

INTERNET RESOURCES

PERFORMING RIGHTS ORGANIZATIONS

ASCAP
www.ascap.com
Excellent resource for performing rights information. Includes online title search facilities.

BMI
www.bmi.com
Contains title search facilities and a great links page to other internet resources.

SESAC
www.sesac.com
Check out their online sample of a television performing rights royalty statement.

COPYRIGHT AND LEGAL INFORMATION

Copyright Office of the Library of Congress
www.lcweb.loc.gov

Copyright Society of the USA
www.csusa.org

ORGANIZATIONS AND ASSOCIATIONS

American Federation of Musicians, Local 47 (Los Angeles area)
www.promusic47.org

Canadian Film Composers Guild
www.goodmedia.com/goodmedia.com/gcfc/index.html

Directors Guild of America
www.dga.org

The Film Music Network
www.filmmusic.net

Film Music Society *(formerly the Society for the Preservation of Film Music)*
www.oldkingcole.com/spfm

The Independent Feature Project
www.ifp.org
Organization of independent film producers and directors

Music Publishers Association of the United States
www.mpa.org

National Music Publishers Association
www.nmpa.org
The Harry Fox Agency, Inc. is found here

Recording Industry Association of America
www.riaa.com

Society for Composers and Lyricists
www.filmscore.org

Songwriters Guild of America
www.songwriters.org

OTHER RESOURCES

Auricle Control Systems
www.auricle.com
Official site for the film music timing management software

East-West Sounds
www.eastwestsounds.com
Great source for digital audio sample CDs

Filmmusic.com
www.filmmusic.com
Good overall information on film scoring and composer sites.

Film Music Magazine
 www.filmmusicmag.com
 Film Music Magazine is a monthly trade publication specifically designed for professionals in the film and television music business. The magazine includes feature articles, industry news, and columns written by industry professionals that address specific areas of the business including audio engineering and technology, marketing, performing rights issues, legal, music editing, music supervision and more.

Filmmaker Magazine
 www.filmmag.com
 Online magazine of independent film. Here you can subscribe to indieWIRE, the daily newswire for the independent film community.

Hollywood Creative Directories
 www.hollyvision.com

Hollywood Online
 www.hollywood.com

The Hollywood Reporter
 www.hollywoodreporter.com
 Excellent source of film and television business news. Features an online version of the magazine and an excellent links page.

Internet Movie Database
 www.imdb.com
 A good place to check out the credits from a film or to make sure your own credits are properly listed.

Kohn Music
 www.kohnmusic.com
 Excellent resource for music licensing information. Extensive links page to various copyright and legal resources. Also has links to foreign performing rights organization sites.

The MIDI Farm
 www.midifarm.com
 MIDI site — lots of links and resources

MIDIMAN
 www.midiman.net
 Manufacturer of MIDI interface products

The Recycler
www.recycler.com
Online classifieds — a great place to look for used gear

INTERNET NEWSGROUPS

Newsgroups are online forums where users share information and views about subjects of interest. We've listed the two that are most relevant to film and television music:

rec.music.movies
A forum with lively discussions about film scores. Keep in mind, however, that most contributors to this forum are fans and critics.
rec.music.compose
This newsgroup is primarily concerned with classical music, but occasionally a discussion of film scoring will appear.

INTERNET MAILING LISTS

Internet mailing lists are similar to newsgroups — they both serve as online forums for discussions. You can choose to receive all messages on a list each day as individual e-mail messages or in *digest* form where the list messages are sent as one large e-mail each day. We recommend the digest form — it's much easier to work with and doesn't clutter up your e-mail in-box.

The Film and Television Music Professionals e-mail discussion list is sponsored by Film Music Magazine and is open to film music professionals and students. To join this list, go to:

www.filmmusicmag.com

Film Music NewsWire and Film Music JobWire are free email services which contain up to the minute information on news of interest to film and television music professionals and employment opportunities in the industry. To sign up for these services, go to the Film Music Magazine website at:

www.filmmusicmag.com

Another list that deals with film and television music is FILMUS-L. Most of the participants on this list are either fans or soundtrack collectors. You can subscribe to FILMUS-L by using your web browser to go to the following web page:

www.netspace.org/cgi-bin/lwgate/FILMUS-L

FINAL THOUGHTS . . .

We hope you have found the materials and ideas presented in this book to be helpful.

Our goal in writing this book is to make practical information available to those entering the business, with the ultimate goal of helping people to be succesful.

We also offer seminars on the film and television music business. To find out the details of our next seminar or to be added to our mailing list, write:

Cinematrax
1146 N. Central Ave. #103
Glendale, CA 91202

or e-mail: info@cinematrax.com

As you build your own career in the film and television music business, we want to wish you the very best of luck and success.

Mark Northam and Lisa Anne Miller

SECTION V
READY-TO-USE FORMS & DOCUMENTS

We have provided several forms and documents that may be useful in your film and television music business. Space has been provided where possible so that you may personalize them with your name, company, and contact information. You may want to consider these forms and documents to be a starting point when designing your own, since every composer's needs are different.

The forms and documents include:

Prospect Information
Music Production Budget
Time Code Work Tape Preparation Instructions (1/2 " Hi-Fi VHS)
Temp Music Work Tape Preparation Instructions (1/2 " Hi-Fi VHS)
Spotting Notes (2 versions)
Master Cue List
Master Cue List Worksheet
Session Checklist
Independent Contractor Agreement
Track Sheet
Recording Session Cue List Worksheet
Final Delivery Cue List (2 versions)
Dubbing Sheet
Studio Inventory

PROSPECT INFORMATION

Date: _____   Source: _____

Project: _____

Contact: _____ Phone: _____

Production Company: _____

Address: _____
_____
Type of Project:

_____
Type of Music Needed:

_____
Important Dates:

_____
Other Notes:

Project:

Date:

Description:

Musicians

Qty	Description	No. of Sessions	Cost per Session	Cartage or Extra Pay	Total Cost
		TOTAL MUSICIAN COSTS			

Creative Costs

Description				Total Cost
		TOTAL CREATIVE COSTS		

Production Costs

Description	No. of Hours	Cost/Hour	Cost/Each	Total Cost
		TOTAL PRODUCTION COSTS		

SUBTOTAL
10%

Contingency

TOTAL PROJECT BUDGET

Notes

TIME CODE WORK TAPE
Preparation Instructions

Please prepare a 1/2" VHS tape as follows:

1. Record all audio except music on to the LEFT (Channel 1) Hi-Fi audio track only. Please reference signal at 0 db.

2. Record audio SMPTE signal on to the RIGHT (Channel 2) Hi-Fi audio track only. <u>Do not record SMPTE on to the analog audio tracks.</u> Please reference signal at -3db and **specify frame rate of time code. (Drop Frame, Non-Drop, etc.)**

3. Prepare window burn of time code that matches with audio SMPTE code.

Please record at least 30 seconds of time code/window burn (pre-roll) before the start of the material and 30 seconds after the end.

TEMP MUSIC WORK TAPE
Preparation Instructions

Please prepare a 1/2" VHS tape as follows:

1. Record all audio/dialogue, including any music from the temp music track on to Hi-Fi channels 1 and 2 (L and R). Please reference signal at 0 db.

2. Prepare window burn of SMPTE concurrent with audio SMPTE code. The time code in the window burn on this tape must match precisely with the time code on any *Time Code Work Tapes* that are being provided for scoring purposes.

SPOTTING NOTES

Project Title _____ Composer _____

Show/Prod. No. _____ Music Editor _____

Episode Title _____ Length of Film/Episode _____

M	
Start Time	
End Time	Total Time
Notes to Composer:	

M	
Start Time	
End Time	Total Time
Notes to Composer:	

M	
Start Time	
End Time	Total Time
Notes to Composer:	

SPOTTING NOTES

Project Title:

Show/Prod. No.:

Episode Title:

Composer:

Music Editor:

Lenth of Film/Episode:

NO.	TITLE	TYPE	LENGTH		SMPTE	CUE PARAMETER DETAILS	SCENE DESCRIPTION AND MUSIC NOTES	OTHER NOTES
			IN	OUT		IN: OUT:		
			IN	OUT		IN: OUT:		
			IN	OUT		IN: OUT:		
			IN	OUT		IN: OUT:		
			IN	OUT		IN: OUT:		
			IN	OUT		IN: OUT:		
			IN	OUT		IN: OUT:		
			IN	OUT		IN: OUT:		
			IN	OUT		IN: OUT:		
			IN	OUT		IN: OUT:		

MASTER CUE LIST

Production Title:

Date:

CUE	TITLE	SMPTE IN	SMPTE OUT	LENGTH

TOTAL BACKGROUND MUSIC	
TOTAL SOURCE	
TOTAL MUSIC	

MASTER CUE LIST WORKSHEET

Production Title:

Date:

CUE	TITLE	TIME		SMPTE		PROGRESS				NOTES
				IN	OUT	WRITE	FIX	REWRITE	APPROVE	

SESSION CHECKLIST

Session:_____ Contact:_____

Location:_____ Phone:_____

Address: _____

Date:_____ Time:_____

_____   Set aside all blank tapes required:

Audio: _____   Qty: _____

_____   Qty: _____

_____   Qty: _____

Video: _____   Qty: _____

_____   Format and and Stripe with Time Code

Instructions:_____

_____

_____   Rent all equipment necessary

Instructions:_____

_____

_____

_____

_____   Make arrangements for Food/Drinks

_____   Confirm Musicians, Engineer and other music personnel

_____   Confirm Studio if necessary

_____   Make sure Clients know the time and place of session

_____   Other:_____

_____

_____

INDEPENDENT CONTRACTOR AGREEMENT

Name and Address:

_____

_____

_____

_____

Social Security Number / Tax ID:_____

I understand and agree that my relationship with _____
will be that of an independent contractor and not an employee. I am responsible for
any and all taxes assessed with respect to compensation paid to me. I understand
that I will receive no residual payments or additional payments or benefits of any
kind other than my direct pay for the recording sessions.

Signed_____ Date:_____

DATE:

PROJECT:

PRODUCTION NO.:

CLIENT:

ENGINEER:

CUE / SONG TITLE:

COMPOSER:

1	2	3	4	5	6	7	8
9	10	11	12	13	14	15	16
17	18	19	20	21	22	23	24

NOTES:

TIMECODE TYPE
❑ 29.97 Non-Drop
❑ Drop frame
❑ Other: _____

	Hour	Minute	Second	Frame
AUDIO TIME CODE START:	__ :	__ :	__ :	__
VIDEO TIME CODE START:	__ :	__ :	__ :	__
TIME CODE OFFSET:	__ :	__ :	__ :	__

RECORDING SESSION CUE LIST WORKSHEET

Production Title:

Date:

CUE #	TITLE	TIME	IN	OUT	INSTRUMENTS	CHTS.	REC.	MIX	NOTES

FINAL MUSIC CUE LIST

Client:
Project:
Date:
Tape Format:

#	CUE	TITLE	TC Start	Approx. Timing	Tape TRACKS	SAFETY DAT TRACK NO.	Notes

FINAL DELIVERY CUE LIST

Production:

Date:

DAT Recorded @   K

Prog ID	Cue #	Cue Title	Length	Notes

STUDIO INVENTORY

MFG	TYPE	DESCRIPTION	SERIAL NO.	PURCHASE PRICE	INSURED VALUE

FILM MUSIC™

the professional voice of music for film and television

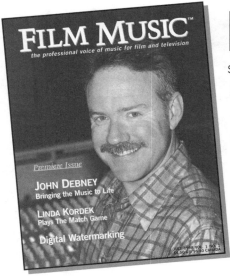

PROFESSIONAL

Film Music magazine is a monthly trade publication specifically designed for professionals in the film and television music business. Each issue includes comprehensive coverage of industry news, feature articles on established and up-and-coming film music personalities, investigative reporting about subjects of concern to film and television music professionals, and a complete calendar of film and television music events.

FEATURES

Film Music magazine also features monthly columns written by industry professionals that address specific areas of the business, including Audio Engineering and Technology, Music Editing, Music Supervision, Marketing, Performing Rights, Multimedia, Legal, the Director's View, Working as a Studio Musician, and a focus on the history of Film Music.

FOCUS

Film Music magazine focuses on news and issues of interest to professionals in the industry, and does not include any critiques, judgments, or criticism of film and television composers or their music.

NETWORK

Film Music magazine also sponsors The Film Music Network, an organization established for professionals in the film and television music business. A subscription to Film Music magazine is included in the member benefits package for all Film Music Network members.

For more information about Film Music magazine visit our web site at **www.filmmusicmag.com**

SUBSCRIBE TO

FILM MUSIC™

the professional voice of music for film and television

There are three easy ways to subscribe...

ONLINE

Subscribe today on the internet. Just go to

www.filmmusicmag.com

BY PHONE

For fastest service call

1-888-678-6158 to order

your subscription today

BY MAIL

Send in the order

form below to begin

your subscription

WOULD LIKE TO SUBSCRIBE TO FILM MUSIC MAGAZINE, PLEASE

❏ Begin my subscription
❏ Renew my subscription

❏ Send me more info about
The Film Music Network

me _____

mpany Name: _____

dress: _____

y/State: _____ Zip/Postal Code: _____

untry: _____

one: _____ Fax: _____

mail address: _____

mary Business: _____

FILM MUSIC MAGAZINE SUBSCRIPTION TYPE:

❏ U.S. Subscriber $29.95/Year
❏ Canada/Mexico Subscriber $35.00/Year
❏ International Subscriber $45.00/Year
(prices subject to change)

METHOD OF PAYMENT:

❏ VISA   ❏ MASTERCARD
❏ Check/Money Order

Credit card number: _____

Expiration Date: _____

Signature: _____

Zip code of billing address for credit card: _____

e: If you are paying by check or money order, please mail the above amount (U.S. funds only) to:

FILM MUSIC MAGAZINE
5000 Eagle Rock Blvd. #107
Los Angeles, CA 90041

Film Music magazine is a publication of the Film Music Publications, LLC. For questions about your subscription call

1-888-678-6158 International 818-507-5377

HL-FTCRG